BLACK DEATHS IN POLICE CUSTODY AND HUMAN RIGHTS

The failure of the Stephen Lawrence Inquiry

DAVID MAYBERRY

D1382448

Published by Hansib Publications in 2008
London & Hertfordshire

Hansib Publications Limited
P.O. Box 226, Hertford, Hertfordshire, SG14 3WY, UK

Email: info@hansib-books.com
Website: www.hansib-books.com

A catalogue record of this book is
available from the British Library

ISBN 978-1-906190-09-5

Printed and bound in the UK

ACKNOWLEDGEMENTS

I WOULD LIKE TO THANK ARIF ALI OF HANSIB PUBLICATIONS and Richard Painter of Print Resources for their help and encouragement in the production of the book. In addition, I would like to thank my parents John and Margaret Mayberry and my brother Huw for their support.

CONTENTS

INTRODUCTION

THE FOCUS OF THIS WORK WAS TO INVESTIGATE whether the police had changed their practices towards Black communities since the Stephen Lawrence Inquiry. The central issue was the problem of Black deaths in police custody and whether the absence of an obvious human rights dimension to the Inquiry and its recommendations had meant that practices had remained unchanged. Some of the key considerations were the commitment of the government and senior police officers to the realisation of the recommendations, their interplay with human rights training and their wider effect on operational policing.

The approach used was to review official data and how this related to the opinions of working police officers. This was considered against the background of the views published by non-governmental organisations, such as Liberty and Inquest. The main conclusion was that the police had not changed their approach to Black people and human rights had continued to be disproportionately infringed.

THE NEED FOR JUSTICE

ON THE EVENING OF 22 APRIL 1993 STEPHEN LAWRENCE was attacked by a group of White youths on Dickson Road, Eltham, South East London. Within a short time he was dead. This was followed by two failed investigations into the circumstances surrounding the Black teenager's death and a failure to prosecute any assailant. This prompted condemnation, not only from the family, but also international statesmen, such as Nelson Mandela.[1]

The Inquiry into the Matters Arising from the Death of Stephen Lawrence[2] has become a cornerstone of British policing. Its verdict of institutional racism, 'the collective failure of an organisation to provide an appropriate and professional service to people because of their colour, culture or ethnic origin'[3] was a damning criticism of the force. These findings generated seventy recommendations which aimed to improve the service delivered by the police. Amongst others these included the titles: openness, accountability and the restoration of confidence; reporting and recording of racist incidents and crimes; police practice and the investigation of racist crime; training for first aid; racism awareness and valuing cultural diversity; stop and search; recruitment and retention and finally prevention and the role of education.[4] Although the Stephen Lawrence Inquiry was not established under the rubric of human rights, its recommendations should contribute to affirming the human rights obligations the police have to fulfil as a public body under the Human Rights Act.[5] Moreover, given the absence of any domestically produced rights based inquiry or document of comparable importance, the realisation of its recommendations provides one way of assessing the development of human rights policies towards minority ethnic groups.

Beyond the immediate relevance the recommendations have for Article 14 of the European Convention on Human Rights (ECHR) and the Human Rights Act,[6] which prohibit all forms of discrimination, it can be seen to have wider implications for other articles. This includes Article 2 of ECHR concerning the right to life and Article 3 prohibiting all forms of torture. In terms of operational policing within Britain, Article 2 has been directly related to protection of life during arrest, use of force, treatment of prisoners in custody and handcuffing.[7] It ultimately deals with death. Article 3 is relevant to the ill treatment of people in custody.[8]

History of ethnic minority groups and the police

The Stephen Lawrence Inquiry was compiled against a background of issues between the police and minority ethnic groups. Tensions between Black communities and the police have been noted since the 1970s[9] and reached their height during the Brixton Disorders of April 1981.[10] According to Lord Scarman's report *The Brixton Disorders: 10-12 April 1981* these were precipitated by Operation Swamp. This was an attempt to reinforce law and order through an overwhelming police presence in Brixton.[11] However, Scarman rejected the notion of institutional racism which he defined as 'practices adopted by public bodies as well as by private individuals who are unwittingly discriminatory against Black people'.[12] Nevertheless the report stated that there were some police officers who were racist.[13] For this reason, it supported a series of changes aimed at encouraging cooperation and confidence between the Black community and the police. In terms of police training, it encouraged greater attention to be paid to cultural awareness in addition to law reform aimed at gaining tighter control over stop and search powers. It also pushed for changes in the training and processes used for detaining and interrogating suspects.[14] Some had felt that these developments brought in a new era of interdependence between the police and the public.[15] Although it had provided the stimulus for the 1984 Police and Criminal Evidence Act (PACE 1984),[16] which legislated on the police complaints system, powers of seizure, entry and search,[17] it formed the backdrop for further tensions. Riots had also taken place in the St. Paul's area of Bristol, Toxteth, Liverpool, Moss Side, Manchester and in Handsworth, Birmingham in 1980 and 1981.[18]

As with the early 1980s, subsequent years witnessed continued problems between the police and minority ethnic groups, particularly over Stop and Search procedures. Much of this was substantiated by studies conducted on behalf of the Home Office concerning the use of stop and search powers by the early 1990s.[19] At this time there was also emerging disquiet about the high incidence of Black deaths in custody[20]. However, these individual issues were rapidly overshadowed by the fallout of the Stephen Lawrence Inquiry in February 1999.[21] Its identification of institutionalised racism placed significant pressure on the police for change. In fact, on February 24 1999, at Prime Minister's Question Time, Tony Blair commented that 'the test of our sincerity as law makers .... is not how well we can express sympathy with the Lawrence family but how well we implement the recommendations to make sure this type of thing never happens in our country again.'[22]

THE PROBLEM – POST STEPHEN LAWRENCE
Police training and recruitment

On paper the recommendations made by the Stephen Lawrence Inquiry would appear to provide solutions to institutional racism. However, within a year of their publication the belief had emerged that these intentions had not been translated into practice.[23] By 2003 the Metropolitan Black Police Association was leading a campaign aimed at discouraging potential recruits from ethnic minority backgrounds following accusations of corruption against a senior Asian officer, Superintendent Ali Desai.[24] Much of this was exacerbated by the BBC documentary, *The Secret Policeman*, which highlighted the continued existence of strands of extreme racism amongst members of the force.[25] There have also been suggestions that the training programmes offered in light of Stephen Lawrence have had limited practical value for day-to-day policing.[26] This is because they have not been linked to needs analysis or staff appraisal.[27]

Treatment of ethnic minorities – deaths in police custody

Problems over recruitment and training are accorded to more specific issues concerning the treatment of members of ethnic minorities by police officers. The use of stop and search powers remains contentious.[28] However, this becomes less of a concern when one considers the more worrying problem of Black deaths in police custody.[29] The emergence of this issue dates back to the 1970s[30] but gathered momentum in the 1980s following the establishment of the non-governmental organisation (NGO), Inquest. Since the 1990s, this has been complemented by a growing body of literature produced by Inquest and other NGOs such as the Institute of Race Relations and Liberty.[31,32] Under the Police and Criminal Evidence Act (PACE), 1984 there are two definitions of a death in custody. The first assumes that an individual had died having been taken to a police station following arrest or that death occurred at a police station which the suspect had voluntarily attended. The second assumes that the deceased was otherwise in the hands of the police or that death resulted from the actions of the police. Possible situations are when the suspect had died whilst being interviewed by the police but had not been detained or when the suspect died whilst actively attempting to evade arrest. Other examples are when the suspect died whilst being stopped and searched or when the suspect died when being questioned by the police or when they died when in a police vehicle, other than whilst in police detention.[33]

Deaths from these circumstances have attracted a heightened response from Liberty and Inquest since the year 2000. The publication of Liberty's 2003 investigation *Deaths in Custody: Redress and Remedies* was a notable case in point.[34] At the time of the Stephen Lawrence Inquiry the Home Office had also provided data confirming Black deaths in police custody were disproportionate with respect to their representation within the population.[35] In fact, statistics collected by Inquest have shown that Black deaths in police custody have remained a consistent problem with numbers relatively much greater than for their White counterparts. Although many of these deaths could be explained, there remains a significant minority where there have been accusations of inadequate investigation by the coroner or no explanation has been made apparent.[36] Under the Human Rights Act, the police, as a public body, have an obligation to uphold human rights as enshrined in the European Convention on Human Rights (ECHR).[37] Whilst all articles within the Act have relevance to police practice, some have arguably greater importance with respect to custody issues. These include Article 2, which protects the right to life, in addition to Article 3, which prohibits torture and inhuman or degrading treatment.[38] In the case of Article 2, this imposes a negative duty on public bodies such as the police to not take life intentionally and a positive duty to protect life. The positive duty has two components. First, it places positive obligations on the detaining authorities to protect individuals whose lives are known to be at risk. Second, it requires the police, coroners, crown prosecutors and other investigating bodies to ensure that deaths in custody are appropriately managed and investigated.[39] As such, the fulfilment of these obligations depends upon issues such as cell design and construction; role and status of custody officers; custody management policies and procedures; assessment and screening procedures as well as training and investigations of deaths in custody.[40]

The problem of Black deaths in custody becomes additionally salient when one considers the Stephen Lawrence Inquiry. Although it was not investigated within a human rights framework, it made practical recommendations which aimed 'to increase trust and confidence in policing amongst minority ethnic communities.'[41] A sizeable number of these recommendations concerned the training of officers. As a result, the Home Office commissioned research which led to the publication of *Training in Racism Awareness and Cultural Diversity*.[42] Nevertheless, the disproportionately high levels of Black deaths in custody and the additional controversies which have surrounded some of these deaths raise questions as to the value of the diversity training programmes undertaken by the police and whether they have any purpose in operational policing. In fact a lack of substance to diversity training as a method for holding the police to account can only be seen to contribute to the arguably invidious relationship which exists between the police and the Crown Prosecution Service, which investigates deaths in police custody.

The question

The Stephen Lawrence Inquiry was seen as a 'turning point' in police–minority ethnic relations. Given the absence of any rights based Inquiry of comparable importance, the realisation of its recommendations provides one way of assessing the development of a human rights policy towards minority ethnic groups. Whilst the Inquiry did not discuss custody issues beyond a cursory level,[43] its recommendations sought to introduce greater racial sensitivity to police training. If effectively integrated into operational policing, these are likely to have had a transferable value for upholding human rights obligations in situations such as custody. So the fundamental questions addressed by this report were:

1. Has the Stephen Lawrence Inquiry meant that the police have changed their practices in respect of the human rights of members of Black communities?
2. Has this been the case with Black deaths in police custody?

THE APPROACH TO THE INVESTIGATION IS OUTLINED BELOW.
Hypothesis

The Stephen Lawrence Inquiry was an opportunity for change within the police. The hypothesis underlying this investigation is that the absence of an obvious human rights dimension to the report and its recommendations contributed to a questionable policy towards members of Black communities and to the problem of Black deaths in police custody.

Methodology

The method of study comprised both qualitative and quantitative analyses. A quantitative element which drew on government and independently collated data provided an understanding of statistical changes in deaths in police custody. The qualitative element comprised an assessment of official custody, human rights and diversity training documents. This allowed an understanding of whether training programmes were sufficient and converged so as to allow the human rights of minority ethnic groups to be specifically considered. It also focused on reports compiled by non-governmental organisations (NGOs) and independent academic researchers. This allowed a more three dimensional critique of the effectiveness of training undertaken since the Lawrence Inquiry. Richness was given to these findings through qualitative semi-structured interviews conducted with police officers. These focused on gaining an appreciation of officers' understanding of diversity training, its relationship to human rights training and its role in operational policing. Accordingly, this permitted an understanding of the extent to which training has had an obvious and transferable purpose for custody issues. Much of this was assessed against a background of instances of deaths in police custody where there have been accusations of the police falling short of human rights obligations. In particular, this drew on cases where the deceased was Black. This provided a structured method for assessing whether diversity training had fulfilled a purpose in sustaining and maintaining the rights of Black people in custody.

Structure

The study progressively moves from a consideration of deaths in police custody to an assessment of the diversity programmes undertaken since the Stephen Lawrence Inquiry. Then, it considers the role of diversity training in upholding the rights of minority ethnic detainees in custody. In conclusion, it makes a series of recommendations that aim to provide more solid ground for diversity training whilst ensuring that more accountable and effective systems for managing and investigating problems in custody are introduced.

Implications of the report

By drawing attention to the problem of Black deaths in police custody this investigation can help illustrate that training in race relations needs to be grounded in more effective systems which are relevant to operational policing and are ultimately accountable. On the other hand, it will look to highlight that the obfuscation and failure which characterised the Metropolitan Police's investigation of Stephen Lawrence's death remain disturbing characteristics of policing in the UK. Though, most importantly it aims to raise awareness of the tragic and little known problem of Black deaths in police custody.

NOTES AND REFERENCES

1. http://www.guardian.co.uk/lawrence/Story/0,,941199,00.html#article_continue
2. Macpherson W *The Stephen Lawrence Inquiry* HMSO (London, 1999)
3. Macpherson *The Stephen Lawrence Inquiry Recommendation* 6.34 p.28
4. Macpherson *The Stephen Lawrence Inquiry* pp. 327 - 335
5. Human Rights Act 1998 HMSO (London, 1998) Section 6
6. Human Rights Act 1998 HMSO (London, 1998) Schedule 1
7. Beckley A *Human Rights. The Pocket Guide for Police Officers and Support Staff.* The New Police Bookshop (Surrey, 2000) p.56
8. Beckley *Human Rights* p.58
9. Bygott D *Black and British* Oxford University Press (Oxford, 1982) p.70
10. Scarman the Lord *The Scarman Report. The Brixton Disorders 10 – 12 April 1981* Penguin Books (Harmondsworth, 1981)
11. Taylor S 'The Scarman Report and explanations of riots' in *Scarman and After. Essays reflecting on Lord Scarman's Report, the riots and their aftermath* ed. Benyon J Pergamon Press (Oxford, 1984) p.28
12. Scarman *The Scarman Report* p.28 point 2.22
13. Scarman *The Scarman Report* p.105 points 4.63
14. Taylor 'The Scarman Report and explanations of riots' p.29
15. Neyroud P & Beckley A *Policing, Ethics and Human Rights* Willan Publishin (Cullompton, 2001)
16. Police and Criminal Evidence Act 1984
17. Rowe M *Policing, Race and Racism* Willan Publishing (Cullompton, 2004) p.83
18. Holdaway *Black or White? The Racialisation of British Policing* Macmillan Press Ltd (Basingstoke 1996) p.111
19. FitzGerald M & Sibbit R *Ethnic Monitoring in Police Forces: a Beginning Research Study* 173 Metropolitan Police (London, 1999) p.41
20. Institute of Race Relations *Deadly Silence. Black Deaths in Custody* Institute of Race

Relations (London, 1991) pp.47 - 9

21. Cathcart B *The Case of Stephen Lawrence* Viking (London, 1999) pp.122 - 3

22. Cathcart *The Case of Stephen Lawrence* p.404

23. Marlow A & Loveday B 'Race, policing and the need for leadership' in *After Macpherson. Policing after the Stephen Lawrence Inquiry.* Ed Marlow A & Loveday B Russell House Publishing (Lyme Regis 2000) p.2

24. Rowe *Policing*, p.25

25. Rowe *Policing*, p.12

26. Rowe *Policing*, p.76

27. Rowe *Policing*, p.77

28. Rowe *Policing*, p.89

29. http://inquest.gn.apc.org/stats_police.html

30. Biles D 'Deaths in custody: the nature and the scope of the problem' in *Deaths in Custody. International Perspectives.* ed. Liebling A & Ward T Whiting & Birch Ltd (London, 1994) p.16

31. Institute of Race Relations *Deadly Silence. Black Deaths in Custody* Institute of Race Relations (London, 1991)

32. Vogt GS & Wadham J *Deaths in Custody: Redress and Remedies* Liberty (2003) http://www.liberty-human-rights.org.uk/resources/articles/pdfs/liberty-inquest-booklet.pdf

33. Police and Criminal Evidence Act 1984 section 118 (2)

34. http://inquest.gn.apc.org/data_black_deaths_in_police_custody.html. There were 37 black and minority deaths in custody between 1994 and 1998 compared to 30 deaths between 2000 and 2004. This compares with 280 white deaths between 1994 and 1998 and 230 between 2000 and 2004.

35. Leigh A Johnson G & Ingram A *Deaths in Police Custody: Learning the Lessons.* Police Research Series Paper 26 ed. Laycock G Home Office (London, 1998) p.51

36. Butler G *Inquiry into Crown Prosecution Service Decision-Making in Relation to Deaths in Custody and Related Matters* The Stationery Office (London, 1999)

37. Starmer K Strange M & Whitaker Q *Criminal Justice, Police Powers and Human Rights.* Oxford University Press (Oxford, 2001) p.13

38. Starmer *Criminal Justice* p.18

39. United Kingdom Parliament *Joint Committee on Human Rights - Third Report* http://www.publications.parliament.uk/pa/jt200405/jtselect/jtrights/15/1502.htm p.13

40. Ure J 'Police accountability in custody management: creating the climate.' In *Deaths in Custody. International Perspectives.* ed. Liebling A & Ward T Whiting & Birch Ltd (London, 1994) p.183

41. Macpherson *The Stephen Lawrence Inquiry* p.327

42. Home Office *Training in racism and cultural diversity* Home Office Development and Practice Report (London, undated)

43. Macpherson *The Stephen Lawrence Inquiry* p.324 point 46.35

DIVERSITY AND THE POLICE.
WHERE HAS IT GONE WRONG?

BY DRAWING ON STUDIES COMPILED BY THE HOME OFFICE, Inquest and other independent researchers, this chapter reviews Black deaths in police custody both before and in light of the Stephen Lawrence Inquiry. It looks at how disproportionate numbers of deaths amongst Black communities can be attributed to weaknesses and lack of purpose to diversity training. This assesses the commitment of the government and senior police officers to fulfilling the Lawrence Inquiry's recommendations. Critically, it considers how this has frustrated attempts to develop an effective and co-ordinated programme for race relations at a force level and has resulted in diversity having little or no consistency with other areas of police training. Most importantly, it looks at how this has resulted in police officers failing to see the relevance of racial awareness to custody situations.

All deaths in police custody are tragic affairs. However, they become increasingly disconcerting when questions are raised about the human rights of the deceased or when there are disproportionate numbers of deaths amongst a particular social group. Between 1994 and 2005 there have been 877 deaths in police custody.[1] Whilst studies have drawn attention to the high number of males who die in custody,[2] the topic of most disturbing interest has been Black deaths. The focus on this has been to such an extent that some organisations have made these cases a specific point of reference and analysis.[3] Although Inquest provided figures demonstrating how disproportionate these numbers are any clear understanding of this prior to 1996 is severely limited because the police did not disclose the ethnic or racial background of the deceased.[4] It was only with the publication of the 1998 Home Office study, *Deaths in Police Custody: Learning the Lessons*, that it is possible to gain some insight into why it was such a problem.[5] Despite commenting that the disproportionately large number of Black deaths in custody can be attributed to the high number of Black people who enter custody,[6] this study drew attention to the large number of deaths which may have resulted from police restraint between 1990 and 1996. This amounted

16

to 7 out of the 19 Black deaths studied (37%), which compared with 9 of 225 White deaths (4%) in police custody.[7] Accordingly, this placed the police at variance with Articles 2 and 3 of the European Convention of Human Rights, whilst the disproportionate number of Black deaths involving restraint would appear to have unavoidable racial overtones. Therefore, it had wider implications for article 14 which states that 'rights and freedoms ... shall be secured without discrimination on any ground such as sex, race, colour, language'.[8]

Black deaths in custody have continued to be a problem since the passage of the Human Rights Act in 1998[9] and the publication of *The Stephen Lawrence Inquiry* in 1999. Statistics collected by the Home Office have shown that of 67 deaths in police custody between mid 1998 and mid 1999, 7 were Black.[10] Whilst this is a crude comparison to make, such a figure is not consistent with the percentage of Black people in the population at the time of the 1991 census.[11] In fact, this particular issue has continued to be a prevalent feature of even the most recent studies compiled by the Home Office. Between April 1999 and March 2000 3 of 70 deaths in custody involved Black people,[12] between mid 2000 and 2001, 7 of 52,[13] between April 2001 and March 2002, 4 out of 70,[14] between April 2002 and March 2003, 17 of 104,[15] and 7 out of 100 between April 2003 and March 2004.[16] Underlying concerns about disproportionate numbers of deaths amongst Black communities were reaffirmed by an additional Home Office study, which specifically investigated minority ethnic deaths in custody.[17] It concluded that, despite their relative youth and lack of mental health problems, Black and minority ethnic deaths were still characterised by higher levels of restraint than those where the detained person was White.[18] This observation does not confirm whether there were any overt infringements of human rights or whether these were failures by the police to operate in a proportionate manner. Nevertheless, it suggested that officers' approach to the detained was different if they were Black or from another minority ethnic group and this was ultimately at the expense of their human rights.

Since 1999, the Stephen Lawrence Inquiry has provided the backdrop to the problem of Black deaths in police custody. However, it is important to understand that the first steps towards realizing its recommendations were hesitant and obtuse. The Home Secretary's Action Plan[19] was produced a year after the publication of the Stephen Lawrence Inquiry. Although it largely accepted the recommendations, it did express some significant reservations. Notably, this included concerns over freedom of information and the prosecution of offences which had taken place somewhere other than a public place.[20] In addition, it failed to develop the recommendations into clear programmes or targets for the police. Instead, it set a broad range of criteria against which success could be measured such as 'establishing partnership and involvement with minority ethnic groups' and the 'raising of standards and promoting of professional competence'.[21] In this way, it reflected a lack of commitment on behalf of central government and a failure to process a rigorous strategy which could be easily appraised.

Concerns about the government's commitment to the Stephen Lawrence Inquiry are consistent with a belief held in some quarters of the academic community that reform programmes had been intentionally drafted in order to be vague and disconnected from the harsh realities of the Inquiry's conclusions.[22] This can be seen in the literature produced by the government concerning diversity training. Although it expanded on the initial recommendations, it did not establish statistical targets against which success could be measured.[23] The government, itself, acknowledged similar problems in the *National Learning Requirement* for diversity training of 2004 which drew attention to Her Majesty's Inspectorate of Constabulary (HMIC) comments on the failure to establish a clearly defined national strategy for diversity training.[24] It is noteworthy that it was only with the advent of *A Strategy for Improving Performance in Race and Diversity 2004 - 2009* that the government appeared to make any explicit link between diversity training and the Human Rights Act which had been introduced in order to hold public bodies such as the police to account.[25] Clearly, the government did not appear to have an immediate and comprehensive response to the Lawrence Inquiry's recommendations, whilst any consideration of human rights seems to have been a peripheral concern until recently.

The failure of the government to establish a structured and extensive response to the Lawrence Inquiry has resonated in the attitude of Chief Constables towards diversity training. *Winning the Race. Embracing Diversity* stated that it is the responsibility of Chief Officers to implement community race relations programmes and diversity training at a force level.[26] However, the Final Report by the Commission on Racial Equality (CRE) in 2005 commented that of the forces they surveyed only two thirds had established a specific diversity training strategy.[27] In contrast, Home Office literature had suggested that 98% of forces had established or were developing some form of strategy to deal with race relations by 2001.[28] There have also been concerns that in the Metropolitan Police Service a line of accountability for the realisation of such programmes has been obscured because it is not structured in the same way as other constabularies in the UK.[29] This is consistent with studies of command in the police, which state that, aside from financial issues, the most significant difficulty chief constables face is maintaining close control over policy.[30] Implicit within this observation is that there would appear to be some problems over the top down realisation of diversity training programmes whilst the accountability of senior officers may be frustrated by a complex and confusing system of organisation.

Problems concerning the accountability of Chief Police Officers become increasingly apparent when one considers the Association of Chief Police Officers (ACPO). This organisation devises the diversity training programmes for implementation at force level.[31] It is important to note that although documents such as the ACPO diversity strategy are available to the public,[32] the organisation's website comments that many of its activities are not generally disclosed. This is possible because it is a private company rather than a public body and, is therefore, not subject to the Freedom of Information Act.[33] The Audit Commission also states that when a public body contracts out service to the private sector it cannot assume that they will be liable for any breach of human rights.[34] Given the Lawrence Inquiry's findings, it would appear necessary to establish an open and accountable system which has obvious links to the internal structure of the police. ACPO has also been seen as a 'loose' organisation which only operates to serve the mutual interests of Chief Officers.[35] Moreover, in 2005 the Commission for Racial Equality (CRE) argued that ACPO needed to develop a more extensive strategy in order to meet the recommendations of the Lawrence Inquiry.[36] Both this lack of clarity and depth make it increasingly possible to question the commitment of senior officers to the Stephen Lawrence Inquiry.

Issues surrounding the creation and implementation of diversity training programmes have filtered into the problems concerning basic command unit (BCU) commanders, who have become increasingly responsible for the day-to-day management of policing.[37] As already implied lines of accountability between Chief Police Officers and officers who operate at a BCU level have been a point of concern.[38] Allied to this has been the problem of 'residual cynicism'. *Winning the Race* drew attention to officers who worked towards the realisation of community race relations programmes and diversity training, but commented that they were marginalised by BCU commanders who exhibited signs of resistance.[39] A consequence of this has been that the work of community relations' officers has been increasingly ignored or rescinded by their superiors.[40] Whilst this example is not directly linked to diversity training, it helps illustrate that poor management can result in failures to fulfill aspirations for improved community and race relations. This has not only been the product of antipathy. An alternative view is that as a result of the restructuring which coincided with the Stephen Lawrence Inquiry, BCU commanders felt blamed for failures in areas in which they had little specialist knowledge.[41] This development suggested that modernisation has become more of a priority for the police than establishing a system for racial awareness which has had significant affects on police practice.

Concerns about diversity and race relations training are not confined to the commitment of senior officers, but also encompass the role of community consultation. Both the ACPO *Race and Diversity Strategy*[42] and the *National Learning Requirement* [43] stress its importance as a component in the creation of effective diversity training programmes. Some forces appear to have actively embraced this strategy. A Home Office investigation commended the efforts of Avon and Somerset and Suffolk constabularies in establishing active links with local Black communities.[44] Additionally, it has been noted that the Metropolitan Police's diversity strategy was conceived with the assistance of members of a wide variety of minority ethnic groups.[45] However, in 2004 the Lawrence Steering Group concluded that although bridges had been established, members of minority ethnic groups still encountered significant hostility and many felt the training has had little visible purpose.[46] This suggested that diversity training was seen as an obligation for the police in the post Stephen Lawrence era rather than something which had been rigorously integrated into operational policing in order to improve the service offered to Black minority ethnic communities.

As well as facing issues surrounding community consultation, there has been criticism of the trainers who deliver the courses. *Training in Racism and Cultural Diversity* emphasises the need for trainers to be carefully chosen in order that they understand the make up of the organisations they are serving, are of both sexes and come from a range of racial backgrounds.[47] At best this advice does not appear to have been obviously embraced by the police. At worst it has fallen on deaf ears. The Central Police Training and Development Authority (Centrex) have reinforced the message of government by producing supplementary guidelines for police forces.[48] However, they have no overall control and much of what happens is at the discretion of individual forces.[49] In addition, many diversity trainers do not receive on-going tuition and are therefore unaware of the implications of changing legislation and systems of accountability.[50] In particular this is likely to include the overhaul of diversity legislation in 2005, the forthcoming single Equality Act and the growing emphasis that the newly created Commission for Equality and Human Rights (CEHR) will place on meeting human rights obligations. The immediate consequences have been that there is a lack of consistency between the programmes offered by different constabularies and the trainers often lack authority within the classroom.[51] This showed how a failure to establish an appropriate framework for diversity strategies can make whatever commitment is shown at lower levels increasingly fruitless.

The extent to which one is able to understand constabularies' failure to establish adequate diversity training programmes is limited by issues surrounding auditing systems. The Home Secretary's *Action Plan* discusses the need to establish this type of mechanism in order to make the police accountable for failures or inconsistencies in diversity training.[52] Other commentators have suggested that this should be reinforced through use of an external auditor.[53] The use of Centrex had been seen as a positive movement towards meeting these suggestions.[54] In fact, by April 2004 a common performance and development review (PDR) had even been established.[55] Yet, the budget set aside for Centrex has been cut by thirty percent since 2005.[56] This illustrated the extent of the police's control over systems of disclosure and the extent to which they can limit any degree of external accountability.

In order to gain a more complete appreciation of diversity it is critical to understand whether it operates in conjunction with other fields of training. The links between diversity and human rights training become particularly important when establishing wider concepts about high levels of Black deaths in custody. Although researchers from within the police have commented about the efforts of the ACPO sub-committees to establish systems for training and the promotion of human rights within the police,[57] it is again worrying that their website does not offer the facility to download such a strategy (ACPO).[58] A detailed investigation of the Home Office website revealed that there appear to be no guidelines about human rights and the police for England and Wales. Whilst this does not mean that the police are inimical to human rights, it is disturbing that they have not produced an easily accessible document available for public viewing. Secondary literature also helps to substantiate any suggestion that diversity does not operate consistently with human rights with these books making only brief allusions to the Stephen Lawrence Inquiry.[59] This situation is surprising given article 14 of the ECHR, which states that all rights should be enjoyed irrespective of race or ethnic background. The advantages of a diversity element to human rights training are difficult to quantify, but are likely to have had a complementary purpose.

The failure to emphasise diversity within human rights training is complemented by the limited amount of official literature which places human rights within the context of diversity training. *The Police Race and Diversity Learning and Development Programme* would appear to be one of the only documents produced at a national level which places human rights within the context of diversity training.[60] At a force level the situation is worse. Only the Sussex Police Authority's diversity strategy makes explicit reference to human rights.[61] Given the Lawrence Inquiry's conclusions concerning institutional racism and the wider issues identified by the Report, it is strange that there is limited literature on the incorporation of human rights into diversity training. More to the point, the failure to integrate this into diversity training becomes increasingly questionable when one considers the continued problem of Black deaths in police custody since the publication of the Inquiry.

The extent of the problem surrounding Black deaths in custody might suggest that the police will be integrating diversity issues into custody training. However, this is not the case. Although custody officer manuals extensively discuss the human rights implications of custody, they make no mention of diversity.[62] The need for this to be integrated into custody training is illustrated by an interesting study conducted by Dr. Joanne Britton.[63] This investigated the introduction of a Help on Arrest Scheme (HOAS) offered to Black people once they had entered custody. This gave the detained the opportunity to call an independent member of the public who would come to the police station and give advice and assistance.[64] Britton concluded that the officers she interviewed did not support the programme. Significantly, they believed that the scheme was not necessary because they felt the custody process was never racialised.[65] Britton argued that this was far from true. A failure to take account of race could result in ignoring particular cultural needs and the wider issues which have surrounded the Black community and the police.[66] Moreover, she stated that the officers believed the presence of the HOAS volunteer undermined case building and took steps to limit the assistance given.[67] Critically this reveals where diversity and human rights training have failed to converge and so limit the promotion of a culture which specifically considers the human rights of Black detainees.

The core issue to the Stephen Lawrence's Inquiry's recommendations was the need to increase trust and confidence in the police by ethnic minorities. Although the significance of the Human Rights Act was not explicitly recognised, it should have formed the basis on which these recommendations were implemented. As such it would have given them integrity, bringing together training in diversity and areas of operational policing, such as custody. In practice they are often seen as separate. Critics have expressed doubts about the levels of leadership shown by chief police officers and BCU commanders. To some degree forces have adopted a 'tick box' approach when dealing with training issues about diversity. The benefits of community consultation have also been undermined by the continued problems which have characterised policing in areas with high concentrations of minority ethnic groups. Again there has been a failure to evaluate the effect of such consultations on police practice, to identify changes and assess their impact on the maintenance of human rights on a day-to-day basis. Studies concerning custody have shown that these issues should have an obvious interdependency and any failure to adequately do so could interfere with the right to liberty and security as enshrined in Article 5 of ECHR.

NOTES AND REFERENCES

1. http://inquest.gn.apc.org/data_deaths_in_police_custody.html
2. Leigh *Deaths* p.8
3. Police Leadership and Powers Unit, Home Office *Analysis of Ethnic Minority Deaths in Police Custody* (Home Office Communications Directorate, 2004)
4. Vogt *Deaths in Custody* p.10
5. Leigh *Deaths*
6. Leigh *Deaths* p.vii
7. Leigh *Deaths* p.58
8. http://conventions.coe.int/Treaty/en/Treaties/Html/005.htm
9. http://www.opsi.gov.uk/ACTS/acts1998/19980042.htm
10. http://police.homeoffice.gov.uk/news-and-publications/publication/operational-policing/deaths1999.pdf?view=Binary p.2

11. http://www.statistics.gov.uk/cci/nugget.asp?id=273

12. Police Leadership and Powers Unit, Home Office *Deaths in Police Custody. Statistics for England and Wales, April 1999 to March 2000* (Home Office, London) p.20

13. Police Leadership and Powers Unit, *Home Office Deaths in Police Custody. Statistics for England and Wales, April 2000 to March 2001* (Home Office, London) p.14

14. Police Leadership and Powers Unit, Home Office *Deaths in Police Custody. Statistics for England and Wales, April 2001 to March 2002* (Home Office, London) p.21

15. Woodcock J Maisels J Hudspith D & Irani D *Deaths during or following Police Contact – Statistics for England and Wales April 2002 – March 2003* (Home Office, London) p.36

16. Police Leadership and Powers Unit, Home Office *Deaths during or following Police Contact–Statistics for England and Wales April 2003 – March 2004* p.47

17. Police Leadership *Analysis* p.1

18. Police Leadership *Analysis* pp.5-9

19. Home Office *Stephen Lawrence Inquiry: Home Secretary's Action Plan* (Home Office, London, 1999)

20. Home Office *Stephen Lawrence Inquiry* p.9 & p.20

21. Home Office *Stephen Lawrence Inquiry* p.1

22. McLaughlin JE & Murji K 'After the Stephen Lawrence Report' *Critical Social Policy* Vol. 19, No. 3, (1999) p.381

23. Home Office *Training in racism and cultural diversity* Home Office Development and Practice Report (London, undated)

24. Stuart M & Cragg R *Race and Diversity Training. National Learning Requirement* (Home Office, London, 2004) p.2

25. Home Office *A Strategy for Improving Performance in Race and Diversity 2004 – 2009. The Police Race and Diversity Learning and Development Programme* (Home Office London 2004) p.12

26. Her Majesty's Inspectorate of Constabulary *Winning the Race: Embracing Diversity* (Home Office, London, 2001) p.viii

27. Commission for Racial Equality *The Police Service in England and Wales. Final Report of a formal Investigation by the Commission for Racial Equality* (Commission for Racial Equality, London, 2005) p.66

28. Home Office *Stephen Lawrence Inquiry: Home Secretary's Action Plan. Second Annual Report on Progress* (Home Office, London, 2001) p.3

29. Her Majesty's Inspectorate of Constabulary *Policing London "Winning Consent" A Review of Murder Investigation and Community & Race Relations Issues in the Metropolitan Police Service* (Home Office, London, 2000) p.155

30. Reiner R *Chief Constables: Bobbies, bosses or bureaucrats?* (Oxford University Press, Oxford, 1992) p.229

31. HMIC *Winning the Race: Embracing Diversity* p.82

32. Association of Chief Police Officers *Policing Diversity Strategy* (ACPO London undated)

33. http://www.acpo.police.uk/about_pages/free.html

34. Audit Commission *Human Rights. Improving Public Service Delivery* (Audit Commission London 2003) p.11 point 23

35. Reiner *Chief Constables* p.279

36. CRE *The Police Service* p.68

37. Davies A 'Change in the UK police service: The costs and dilemmas of restructured managerial roles and identities' *Journal of Change Management* Vol. 1 (2000) p.50

38. HMIC *Winning the Race: Embracing Diversity* p.3

39. HMIC *Winning the Race: Embracing Diversity* p.19

40. HMIC *Winning the Race: Embracing Diversity* p.19

41. Davies 'Change in the UK police service' p.51

42. Association of Chief Police Officers *ACPO Business Strategy Race and Diversity Strategy* (ACPO London 2003) p.3

43. *Stuart Race and Diversity Training* p.5

44. Jones T & Newburn T *Widening Access: Improving Police Relations with Hard to Reach Groups* Police Research Series Paper 138 (Home Office, London 2001) p.51

45. Jones T & Newburn T *Widening Access: Improving Police Relations with Hard to Reach Groups* Police Research Series Paper 138 (Home Office, London 2001) p.51

46. HMIC *Policing London* p.51

47. Home Office *Lawrence Steering Group 5th Annual Report 2003 – 2004* (Home Office London 2004) p.16

48. Home Office *Training in racism* p.6

49. http://www.centrex.police.uk/cps/rde/xchg/SID-3E8082DF-B84588E3/centrex/root.xsl/home.html

50. CRE *The Police Service* p.26

51. CRE *The Police Service* p.75

52. Home Office *Stephen Lawrence Inquiry. Home Secretary Action's Plan. Second Annual Report on Progress* (Home Office London 2001) p.30

53. Home Office *Action's Plan* p.3

54. McLaughlin 'After the Stephen Lawrence Report' p.382

55. Home Office *Stephen Lawrence Inquiry: Home Secretary's Action Plan. Third Annual Report on Progress* (Home Office, London, 2002) p.9

56. Home Office *Lawrence Steering Group 5th* p.12

57. CRE *The Police Service* p.85

58. Neyroud *Policing* pp. 205-14

59. http://www.acpo.police.uk/about_pages/free.html

60. Neyroud *Policing* p.50

61. Home Office *A Strategy for Improving Performance*

62. http://www.sussex.police.uk/about_us/race_equality_scheme/SussexPolice Diversity Strategy.pdf

63. Smart H Blackstone's *Custody Officer's Manual* (Oxford University Press, Oxford, 2006)

64. Britton N J 'Race and policing: A study of police custody' *British Journal of Criminology* Vol. 40 (2000) pp. 639-658

65. Britton 'Race and policing' p.642

66. Britton 'Race and policing' p.644

67. Britton 'Race and policing' p.645

68. Britton 'Race and policing' p.652

BLACK DETAINEES: NO RIGHTS?

THIS CHAPTER LOOKS TO EXPLAIN, PRINCIPALLY THROUGH Black deaths in police custody, the extent to which the Stephen Lawrence Inquiry should have been based on human rights. It begins by looking at how concerns about custody are complemented by additional controversies surrounding 'stop and search' procedures. It considers how this can be attributed to the fact that 'diversity' training is nebulous and, therefore, has had a limited impact on officers' approach to operational policing. It then looks at police restraint and limited first aid provision as problems which have characterized Black deaths in police custody. Consideration is given to how this could be due to the absence of purpose in diversity training. Ultimately, it looks at how the lack of accountability to 'diversity' has failed to overcome the close relationship which exists between the police and Crown Prosecution Service, which could limit the potential for justice following a death in police custody.

Alongside Black deaths in custody, the most heavily discussed issue since the publication of the Stephen Lawrence Inquiry has been the use of Stop and Search powers. In terms of operational policing, the appropriate use of this power must take account of Article 5 of the ECHR, the right to liberty and security, and Article 8 concerning the right to privacy.[1] The Stephen Lawrence Inquiry stated that the police needed to become increasingly accountable for the use of these powers. It recommended that all Stops and Searches should be recorded and the police authorities must undertake publicity campaigns to ensure public awareness of the right to receive a record of the episode.[2] Nevertheless, Stop and Search has consistently involved disproportionately large numbers of Black people. Home Office figures for the years 1999 to 2003 suggested that Black people were eight times more likely to be stopped and searched than White people.[3] Some have argued that this is the product of the high concentrations of minority ethnic people who live in areas with high crime rates. They have also suggested that this can be attributed to large numbers of Black people who congregate in urban areas.[4] Yet, since the Inquiry the Home Office stated that there had often been a failure to meet criteria for reasonable suspicion of criminal activity.[5] A follow-up to pilot schemes launched in light of the Stephen Lawrence Inquiry expressed concerns that the systems used to increase accountability were undermined by a lack of consensus amongst officers as to what constituted a Stop and Search.[6] Organisations representing Black interests have also stated that the majority of people are generally unaware of their right to receive a record after having been stopped and searched.[7] Since the extension of these powers under the Terrorism Act 2000, it has been noted that the increase in Stops and Searches for Black and Asian people has been disproportionate. In the Metropolitan Police area there has been a 455% increase in Stops and Searches of Black people in comparison to 488% for Asians and 400% for White people.[8] Evidently, the right to privacy is being disproportionately infringed with respect to minority ethnic groups.

Concerns expressed over Stop and Search are consistent with wider criticisms of diversity. Diversity experts have suggested that although police officers may be aware of diversity, they may not know how to respond to that awareness.[9] An *Interim Report Evaluation of a Diversity Training Programme* in Bexley Borough noted that more than 80% of officers believed the training was worthwhile and had a purpose in providing knowledge and awareness of discrimination. Still, over 70% felt this would not affect the way in which they selected people for Stop and Search and how they subsequently conducted this procedure.[10] According to Kirkpatrick's hierarchy of evaluation this training programme, therefore, failed to achieve the higher learning outcomes of applying newly achieved skills or knowledge (level 3) or having an impact in the community (level 4).[11] In this instance, at least, the purpose of diversity training was little more than fulfilling a government requirement.

These concerns were born out by the interviews I conducted with police officers.[12] The apparent absence of an effective police diversity strategy and the additional problems which have already been identified meant that it was critical to investigate the nature of training that police officers actually received. A schedule of questions was developed to be used in a semi-structured interview.[13] This allowed the sequence of questions to be varied and answers amplified.[14] It also gave me the opportunity to investigate whether there was any evidence of an extensive and uniform diversity training strategy by looking for recurrent use of specific words, phrases or concepts. In addition it allowed an assessment of whether this training had been integrated into operational policing. When questioned, all officers recognised the concept of diversity and stated that they had experienced diversity training. All described its purpose as increasing awareness or understanding. All commented that they had received training from male and female trainers whilst half stated that they had been exposed to trainers who were both internal and external to the police. This would appear to confirm that 'diversity' is an active part of police training and that constabularies are taking some account of community opinions and perspectives. However, when questioned about the purpose of 'diversity' within operational policing they became increasingly hesitant. In particular, the younger officers were not expansive whilst one believed that 'diversity' training had no residual value for her work.[15] These interviews confirmed that training had not been delivered in a way which was consistent with achieving higher learning outcomes and, therefore, rendered expansion on the initial schedule of questions increasingly pointless.

Elements of the wider police family also acknowledge weaknesses in diversity. *Police Review* magazine criticized it because it was not obviously linked to human rights.[16] Again these shortcomings were evident in the interviews.[17] No officer stated explicitly that human rights and diversity training were interdependent. The significance of this can be more clearly discerned when one considers the final question which dealt with custody and its relationship with diversity. Here officers gave vague answers and did not allude to procedures to deal with minority ethnic detainees, apart from generalisations about dietary requirements and prayer. This did not take account of the racial issues identified by the Stephen Lawrence Inquiry, let alone an acknowledgement of the problems which have been associated with the treatment of minority ethnic and Black people in custody. Alarmingly, half of the officers seemed unsure as to whether they had received any human rights training, whilst one was certain that she had not.

"No not really. We've got a mnemonic that we use called PLAN which is proportionate legal um Oh you're testing me now proportionate legal and I can't remember what the A and the N stands for."[18]

The failure of human rights to operate with diversity and custody training provides a disturbing back-drop to Black deaths in custody. The Joint Committee on Human Rights has, itself, acknowledged that custody training is poor and that despite the existence of the Centrex national training programme its implementation depends upon individual constabularies.[19] At the time of the Stephen Lawrence Inquiry Inquest submitted a report stressing the issue of Black and minority deaths in custody.[20] It followed an earlier submission to the United Nations Committee on the Elimination of all Forms of Racial Discrimination.(CERD)[21] These drew attention to the disproportionate number of Africans and African-Caribbeans dying in custody and suggested that the suspicious circumstances which surrounded their deaths were the result of racism within the police and racially motivated violence.[22] One case which was emphasised was that of Shiji Lapite, who died in 1994. He had been stopped by police officers for acting suspiciously. In court they admitted to kicking and biting him. The coroner's verdict was asphyxia which resulted from compression to the neck due to application of a neck hold.[23] Despite these findings there were no prosecutions.[24] This has continued to be a problem since the publication of the Stephen Lawrence Inquiry. A prominent example is the death of Michael Powell in 2003. He was hit by a police car and subsequently arrested. The precise circumstances surrounding his death are unclear and there is uncertainty as to whether it was the result of asphyxia or a heart attack. Regardless, ten police officers were charged with a range of offences associated with his death, but subsequently acquitted.[25, 26] Moreover, between 1991 and 2006 7 of 12 unlawful killings were Black.[27] This confirms that the right to life of Black people, which is embodied in Article 2 of ECHR, is being disproportionately infringed.

In order to gain a more extensive appreciation of the racialisation of deaths in custody, it is critical to understand the role of restraint. Restraint includes unsafe practices, such as holding the detainee face down for prolonged periods.[28] The Joint Committee on Human Rights has suggested that prolonged periods of restraint in the prone position may lead to death and should be restricted to as little as three minutes.[29] This compares with the 20 minutes of restraint which led to brain damage and a fatal cardiac arrest in the case of Roger Sylvester in 1999.[30] A more recent case is that of Paul Coker, who died in the early hours of 6 August 2005 in a police cell in Plumstead, London.[31] Although the post-mortem failed to identify a specific pathology, it has been strongly suggested that restraint was the primary cause of death. Following an investigation by the Independent Police Complaints Commission the case is now with the Crown Prosecution Service.[32] Significantly, these deaths occurred against a background of literature which sought to reduce the risks presented by custody. *Deaths in Police*

Custody: Reducing the Risks drew attention to the problem of restraint and supported an improvement in training for custody and police officers.[33] *Deaths in Police Custody: the risks reduced one year on* commented that, although there were some general improvements, only 63% of constabularies had custody training.[34] By 2004 the government still had no details from the police on the implementation of such training.[35] Given what is known about restraint this adds an even more disturbing dimension to police accountability for deaths in custody.

In addition to restraint other police actions or absence of them have contributed to deaths. In a Home Office study of the twenty six category 3 deaths in custody between 1998 and 2003 the majority were Black or of mixed race. Areas of concern surrounding these deaths included problems associated with positioning during transport, failure to carry out adequate risk assessments and failure to regularly check detainees in custody.[36] The death of Kwame Wiredu was a case in point. In 2002 he was arrested outside a supermarket. On arrest he complained of difficulty with breathing, which was later supported by CCTV evidence.[37] However, about 3 hours after a clinical review by a forensic physician he was found dead.[38] Incidents such as this have not only raised issues about officers working in custody suites but have also reflected on wider structures and systems of accountability. There have been suggestions that some commanding officers have done little more than admonish those involved in unexpected deaths.[39] In some cases this may point towards a systematic form of human rights abuse in which concerns about detainees are outweighed by the need to preserve a constabulary's integrity. As such, they have disturbing parallels with the Metropolitan Police's investigation of Stephen Lawrence's death.

The lack of consideration for positive human rights obligations can be more clearly understood when one assesses the role of First Aid. The Stephen Lawrence Inquiry recommended that First Aid training for police officers should be improved.[40] ACPO has produced guidelines which place First Aid training within the context of the Human Rights Act and the Stephen Lawrence Inquiry.[41] However, it is the responsibility of police forces to implement the strategy ACPO proposed. Importantly training programmes still only lasted for one day as recently as 2005.[42] Up until 2004 problems which were highlighted included failures of officers to attempt resuscitation and a failure to take appropriate action prior to the arrival of the forensic physician or ambulance.[43] A much cited case has been that of Christopher Alder, who died after he had been taken into custody following a fight outside a night club. Police Officers were indifferent to his condition in the custody suite where he was collapsed on the floor struggling to breathe. His deterioration was recorded on CCTV, but there is little evidence to suggest that he was being watched.[44] Again, this shows that even when precautions had been taken to reduce the risks presented by custody, negligence was the product of inadequate training.

Problems surrounding deaths in custody are not confined to issues of treatment and neglect. They also encompass the judicial system through which redress is sought. Until 2004 there had been criticism of the police's control of case referral to the coroner.[45] The Coroner's Act (1988)[46] had failed to make an inquest into a death in police custody mandatory, although in practice it had been accepted as the convention. Since then, the investigation of deaths in custody has fallen under the control of the Independent Police Complaints Commission (IPCC).[47] However, the police still have an element of control over evidence disclosure and the coroner does not yet have an independent investigative branch.[48] Accordingly, this continued influence could lead to lesser verdicts.

Apart from concerns over the police's role in the coroner's process there have been criticisms of the mechanisms leading up to a decision to prosecute. This is currently the responsibility of the Crown Prosecution Service (CPS). It was only in 2003 that this role was more clearly delineated following a review by the Attorney General.[49] As a result, the CPS is obliged to have early contact with families of victims and make them aware of continuing developments. However, the degree of disclosure is limited because of the possibility that family members may be witnesses.[50] Additionally, access to professional legal advice through Legal Aid is technically available, but severely limited.[51, 52] In contrast the CPS provides early and extensive advice to the police.[53] Theoretically this could prejudice the case and again adds weight to the need of public bodies to be more responsive to the community.

Wider limitations of the coronial system have only been recently recognised by the government. Prior to this the system had long been criticized by independent commentators. This not only included NGOs, such as Inquest[54] and Liberty,[55] but also legal textbooks concerned with coronial procedures.[56] Inquest's submission to the Fundamental Review on death certification in England and Wales[57] commented that a majority of families, who had experienced bereavement and a subsequent coronial investigation, had lost confidence in the criminal justice system (87%), the police (70%) and coroners' courts (69%).[58] It drew attention to poor communication, limited disclosure and multiple post mortems.[59] In response, the government's position paper suggested a broad series of changes aimed at increasing independence, professionalism and transparency.[60] The government's draft bill on coronial reform proposes systems of governance, which may improve standards of practice and allow greater uniformity.[61] Although there is provision for appeals against the verdict on cause of death and a proposal for a Charter for the Bereaved,[62] these largely fail to take account of issues to do with the legal assistance given to the police by the CPS in controversial cases. This shows that despite movements towards reform there is still an inadequate consideration amongst policy makers as to the specific issues which surround deaths in custody.

Beyond the coroners' system there have been additional criticisms of the CPS when dealing with verdicts of unlawful killing. The decision to prosecute depends upon a realistic prospect of winning and whether this would be in the public interest.[63] This includes considerations as to the credibility of witnesses and the reliability of evidence. During the consultations that led to a review of the role of the CPS in cases arising from deaths in custody it was suggested that juries seldom doubted the evidence of police officers, although it was rejected in the final report.[64] Meanwhile, the Joint Committee on Human Rights stated that of nine deaths in custody since 1990 there had been only one prosecution and that had been unsuccessful. The Committee also recognised families' distrust of the CPS.[65] In order to sustain public confidence in the system it is therefore important that legislation and court proceedings take more explicit account of the role of police witnesses and defendants. Otherwise such procedures can only be seen to contribute to the infringement of the family's right to a fair trial.

The problems which surround the Black community and the police since the publication of the Stephen Lawrence Inquiry have clear human rights implications. At the same time, the diversity strategies which were introduced in light of the Inquiry's recommendations have not only been poorly implemented, but officers do not believe they have any purpose. Diversity training and human rights training are unrelated and there is evidence suggesting that sections of the force may not have any understanding of human rights. The consequences of this can be seen in the problems surrounding Black deaths in custody. Racial overtones have overshadowed some of these deaths, whilst officers appear unaware of what to do in order to uphold positive human rights obligations. Issues of inadequate first aid provision can be seen as a direct consequence of failing to meet the Inquiry's recommendations. The failure to establish links between human rights and diversity training can also be seen to contribute to a coronial system which operates in the interests of the police. Indeed, movements towards improving this system seem to disregard the role of the police within society, their relationship with minority ethnic communities and the need to provide the family of the deceased with appropriate legal assistance. In short, the confidence of Black people in the police appears to have been systematically undermined as a result of disproportionate and significant human rights infringements.

NOTES AND REFERENCES

1. Beckley *Human Rights* p.26
2. Macpherson *The Stephen Lawrence Inquiry* ch.47 point 61.
3. Qureshi F & Farrell G 'Stop and search in 2004: a survey of police officer views and experiences' *International Journal of Police Science and Management* http://hdl.handle.net/2134/779 p.9
4. Waddington PAJ Stenson K & Don D 'In proportion. Race, and Police Stop and Search' *British Journal of Criminology* Vol. 44 (2004) pp.907-8
5. Quinton P Bland N & Miller J *Police Stops, Decision-making and Practice* Police Research Series Paper 130 (Home Office, London, 2000) p.46
6. Metropolitan Police Authority *Stop and Search: A Community Evaluation of Recommendation 61 in the London Borough of Hackney* (The 1990 Trust 2004) p.34
7. MPA *Stop and Search* p.35 118 MPA *Stop and Search* p.16
8. Clements P *Policing a Diverse Society* (Oxford University Press, Oxford 2006) p.157
9. Ampah T Azah J Hills A Rhoden G & Riley C *Interim Report Evaluation of the Diversity Training Programme Bexley Borough* http://www.met.police.uk/diversity/PDF/ Bexley%20 Interim%20Report.pdf#search=%22Home%20Office%20Purpose %20of%20Diversity%20Training%22 pp.29-30
10. Brookfield SD *Understanding and Facilitating Adult Learning* (Open University Press, Milton Keynes, 1986) p.272
11. See Annexe for transcripts
12. See Annexe for Schedule
13. Bryman A *Social Research Methods* (Oxford University Press, Oxford, 2004) p.113
14. Transcription 3
15. 'Diversity drive "not motivated" by human rights' *Police Review* April 2001 p.14
16. See Transcriptions
17. Transcription 1
18. House of Lords & House of Commons *Joint Committee on Human Rights* – Third Report Session 2004 –05 http://www.publications.parliament.uk/pa/jt200405 /jtselect/jtrights/15/1502.htm pt.259
19. Inquest *Deaths of Black, Minority and Ethnic People in Custody. Inquest's Submission to the*

Stephen Lawrence Inquiry 1998 (Inquest, London, 1998) http://inquest.gn.apc.org /pdf/Deaths_of_Black_Minority_and_Ethnic_People_in_Custody_1998.pdf

20. Inquest *Racial discrimination and deaths in custody: report to the United Nations Committee on the Elimination of all Forms of Racial Discrimination* (CERD). (Inquest, London, 1996)

21. Lords & Commons *Joint Committee on Human Rights* p.1

22. Inquest *Deaths of Black* p.3

23. Butler *Inquiry into Crown Prosecution Service* Section 5

24. Inquest *Criminal Trial of 10 West Midlands Police Officers* Press Release 5 May 2006 http://www.inquest.org.uk/

25. Inquest *Family devastated after acquittal of police officers in Mikey Powell case* Press Release 2 August 2006 http://www.inquest.org.uk/

26. Inquest *Unlawful killing verdicts and prosecutions* http://www.inquest.org.uk/138 Police Complaints Authority *Safer Restraint* (Police Complaints Authority, London, 2002) p.8

27. House of Lords & House of Commons *Joint Committee on Human Rights Deaths in Custody Third Report. Volume 1 Session 2004 – 05* (The Stationery Office, London 2004) http://www.parliament.the-stationeryoffice.co.uk/pa/jt200405/jtselect/jtrights/15 /15.pdf#search=%22Deaths%20in%20custody%22 p.71

28. Inquest *Annual Report 2004* (Inquest London 2004)

29. Inquest Paul Coker *Another death in Metropolitan Police Custody* Press Release 22 August 2005 http://inquest.gn.apc.org/pdf/2005/Paul%20Coker%20INQUEST%20 statement%20August%202005.pdf

30. http://www.ipcc.gov.uk/pr020806_coker.htm

31. Police Complaints Authority *Deaths in Police Custody: Reducing the risks* (Police Complaints Authority, London, 1999)

32. Police Complaints Authority *Deaths in Police Custody: the risks reduced one year on* (Police Complaints Authority, London, 1999)

33. http://www.parliament.the-stationery-office.com/pa/jt200405/jtselect/jtrights/15 4030102.htm

34. Police *Leadership Analysis of Ethnic Minority* pp.6-7

35. Inquest *Kwame Wiredu: Black Death in Stoke Newington: Inquest begins.* Press Release Tuesday 11 October 2005 http://inquest.gn.apc.org/pdf/2005/Kwame_Wiredu_ Inquest_begin_PR_111005.pdf#search=%22Black%20%2B%20Stoke%20 Newington%20%2B%20death%22

36. Police Leadership *Analysis of Ethnic Minority* p.9

37. Police Leadership *Analysis of Ethnic Minority* pp.6-7

38. Macpherson *The Stephen Lawrence Inquiry* Recommendations 45-47

39. ACPO *Report and Recommendations on Police First Aid Training* (ACPO, London, 2001)

40. Home Office *Lawrence Steering Group 6th Annual Report 2005* (Home Office London 2005) p.32

41. Police Leadership *Analysis of Ethnic Minority* p.7

42. Inquest *Death in Police Custody. Report on the death of Christopher Alder. Humberside Police*

1998 (Inquest, London, 2004) http://www.inquest.org.uk/ p.2

43. Dorries C *Coroner's Courts. A Guide to Law and Practice* (Wiley, Chichester, 1999) p.180

44. The Coroner's Act (1988)

45. Crown Prosecution Service *Deaths in Custody – the role of the Crown Prosecution Service* (CPS Communications Branch, London, undated) p.5

46. Vogt *Deaths in Custody* p.42

47. Goldsmith, Lord *A Review of the Role and Practices of the Crown Prosecution Service in Cases Arising from a Death in Custody* (2003) http://www.lslo.gov.uk/pdf/deathincustody.pdf

48. CPS *Deaths in Custody* p.9

49. Vogt *Deaths in Custody* p.46

50. http://www.publications.parliament.uk/pa/cm200506/cmhansrd/cm060508/text/60508w30.htm#60508w30.html_spnew0

51. Goldsmith *A Review* p.17 164 http://www.inquest.org.uk/

52. Vogt *Deaths in Custody* 166 Dorries *Coroner's Courts*

53. Luce T *Death Certification and Investigation in England, Wales and Northern Ireland – The Report of a Fundamental Review 2003* (The Stationery Office, London 2003) http://www.archive2.official-documents.co.uk/document/cm58/5831/5831.htm

54. Inquest *How the Inquest System fails bereaved people. Inquest's Response to the Fundamental Review of Coroner Services* (Inquest, London, 2002) http://inquest.gn.apc.org/pdf/how_the_inquest_system_fails_bereaved_people.pdf p.4

55. Inquest *How the Inquest System fails* pp. 8-15

56. Home Office *Reforming the Coroner and Death Certification System. A Position Paper.* (The Stationery Office, Norwich, 2004) http://www.archive2.official-documents.co.uk/document/cm61/6159/6159.pdf

57. Department for Constitutional Affairs *Coroner Reform: The Government's Draft Bill. Improving Death Investigation in England and Wales* (Department of Constitutional Affairs, London, 2006) http://www.dca.gov.uk/legist/coroners_draft.pdf pp. 58-62

58. DCA *Coroner Reform* p.119-123

59. Goldsmith *A Review* p.30

60. Goldsmith *A Review* p.14 6.3

61. Lords & Commons *Joint Committee 2004 – 05* pp. 97-8

STEPHEN LAWRENCE:
A PYRRHIC VICTORY

IT IS EASY TO LOOK BACK AND SAY ONE COULD HAVE done better, but it is not difficult to see the Stephen Lawrence Inquiry as a Pyrrhic victory for Black and minority ethnic groups. The tragedy and injustice uncovered by the Inquiry should have provided the stimulus for significant changes in police practice whilst visibly challenging a culture which had been branded institutionally racist. However, the Inquiry's recommendations were structurally undermined by a lack of commitment by the government and senior police officers. This led to inadequate training programmes and limited auditing. Consequently officers appear unable to assimilate diversity training into their every day work.

The ineffectiveness of diversity training and its limited impact on police officers goes a long way to explaining problems which have continued to disproportionately affect Black communities. Stop and Search remains the most cited. Yet, deaths in police custody are the most disturbing. Disproportionate levels of restraint identified by both Home Office research and independent watchdogs only help to justify the need for race relations programmes to be grounded in more effective and accountable systems. Indeed, this becomes ever more salient when one considers the close relationship which exists between the police and the Crown Prosecution Service which prosecutes deaths in police custody.

In October 2007, the Commission for Equality and Human Rights (CEHR) will become active. By bringing together the work of the Disability Rights Commission (DRC), the Equal Opportunities Commission (EOC) and the Commission for Racial Equality (CRE), it will look to ensure that public bodies, such as the police, meet their obligations under the Human Rights Act. Black deaths in police custody and issues, such as Stop and Search, should fall within the radar of CEHR. These problems characterised the post Scarman era. They have continued into the post Stephen Lawrence era and have provided the backdrop to the final days of the Commission for Racial Equality (CRE). For this reason, it is critical that more accountable and transparent systems, which rest on a rigorous integration of human rights into operational policing, are introduced. This will identify instances where, at one extreme, there have been systematic failures to uphold human rights and at the other to absolve officers of unwarranted criticism. Failures at all levels to meet the recommendations of the Stephen Lawrence Inquiry mean that it is critical to develop a system which has a free flow of information and responsibility both up and down the command structure of the police.

AN AGENDA FOR CHANGE
The Human Rights Act

It is unlawful for a public body to act in a way which is incompatible with a Convention right.[1] Although there is case law expanding upon this,[2] the Human Rights Act does not discuss how public bodies are to operate so as be complicit. It would, therefore, appear important to give expansion and clarification within the legislation so that human rights accountability can be more clearly defined. This might include a legal requirement for police officers to carry literature which lists their human rights obligations along with their warrant card.

A human rights commission for the police

Although there is a Select Committee, the Joint Committee on Human Rights,[3] public bodies, such as the police, are widespread in their activities and arguably warrant the creation of their own advisory bodies to deal with specific human rights issues. This type of organisation could provide a forum for complaints against the police, such as deaths in police custody. It might also allow more appropriate consideration of issues such as custody and the role of Article 14 of ECHR within operational policing.

The role of senior police officers and chief constables

The Stephen Lawrence Inquiry made Chief Constables responsible for the realisation of its recommendations.[4] The problems which have surrounded their commitment to implementing training programmes and the extent to which this has affected operational policing mean it is important that they become increasingly responsible for any failures.

Aptitude tests and screening for human rights

This is critical for entry into the police force and should be on-going so that suitability is revalidated. Officers who repeatedly fail these assessments should enter a remedial programme and if there is no improvement their employment should be reviewed.

Human rights training

Following initial human rights training there should be refresher courses in order to ensure that officers do not fail to meet human rights obligations during operational activities. This training must reach levels 3 and 4 of the Kirkpatrick model for effective learning.[180]

Stop and Search procedures

Giving a record of the procedure to the suspect should be mandatory. It should include the reasons for the Stop and Search, what happened and its duration. These data should be recorded centrally to identify disproportional practices.

Custody

All custody officers should receive tailored human rights training in order to ensure positive and negative obligations are met. This must occur before a post is taken up as at present this is not always the case.[6]

NOTES AND REFERENCES

1. Human Rights Act (1998) 6i
2. Audit Commission *Human Rights* p.6
3. Feldman D *Civil Liberties and Human Rights in England and Wales* (Oxford University Press, Oxford, 2002) p.94
4. Macpherson *The Stephen Lawrence Inquiry* Recommendation 11
5. Brookfield *Understanding* p.272
6. Lords & Commons *Joint Committee on Human Rights* point 259

BIBLIOGRAPHY

Ampah, T, Azah, J, Hills, A, Rhoden, G, and Riley, C, *Interim Report Evaluation of the Diversity Training Programme Bexley Borough*, http://www.met.police.uk/diversity/PDF/Bexley%20Interim%20Report.pdf#search=%22Home%20Office%20Purpose%20of%20Diversity%20Training%22

Association of Chief Police Officers ACPO, *Report and Recommendations on Police First Aid Training*, (ACPO, London, 2001).

Association of Chief Police Officers (ACPO), *Business Strategy Race and Diversity Strategy*, (ACPO London 2003).

Association of Chief Police Officers, *Policing Diversity Strategy*, (ACPO London undated).

Audit Commission, *Human Rights. Improving Public Service Delivery*, (Audit Commission London, 2003).

Beckley, A, *Human Rights. The Pocket Guide for Police Officers and Support Staff*. The New Police Bookshop (Surrey, 2000).

Biles, D, 'Deaths in custody: the nature and the scope of the problem' in *Deaths in Custody. International Perspectives*. ed. Liebling, A, and Ward, T, Whiting and Birch Ltd (London, 1994) pp. 14–27.

Britton, N. J, 'Race and policing: A study of police custody', *British Journal of Criminology*, Vol. 40 (2000) pp. 639 – 658.

Brookfield, S. D, *Understanding and Facilitating Adult Learning* (Open University Press, Milton Keynes, 1986).

Bryman, A, *Social Research Methods*, (Oxford University Press, Oxford, 2004).

Butler, G, *Inquiry into Crown Prosecution Service Decision-Making in Relation to Deaths in Custody and Related Matters*, The Stationery Office (London, 1999).

Bygott, D, *Black and British*, Oxford University Press (Oxford, 1982).

Cathcart, B, *The Case of Stephen Lawrence* Viking (London, 1999).

Clements, P, *Policing a Diverse Society*, (Oxford University Press, Oxford 2006).

Commission for Racial Equality, *The Police Service in England and Wales. Final Report of a formal Investigation by the Commission for Racial Equality,* (Commission for Racial Equality, London, 2005).

Crawshaw, R, Devlin, B, and Williamson, T, *Human Rights and Policing. Standards for Good Behaviour and a Strategy for Change,* Kluwer Law International (The Hague, 1998).

Davies, A, 'Change in the UK police service: The costs and dilemmas of restructured managerial roles and identities' *Journal of Change Management* Vol. 1 (2000) pp. 41–58

Department for Constitutional Affairs, *Coroner Reform: The Government's Draft Bill. Imroving Death Investigation in England and Wales,* (Department of Constitutional Affairs, London, 2006) http://www.dca.gov.uk/legist/coroners_draft.pdf

'Diversity drive "not motivated" by human rights', *Police Review,* April 2001 p.14.

Dorries, C, *Coroner's Courts. A Guide to Law and Practice,* (Wiley, Chichester, 1999).

Feldman, D, *Civil Liberties and Human Rights in England and Wales,* (Oxford University Press, Oxford, 2002).

FitzGerald, M, and Sibbit, R, *Ethnic Monitoring in Police Forces: a Beginning,* Research Study 173 Metropolitan Police (London, 1999).

Goldsmith, Lord, *A Review of the Role and Practices of the Crown Prosecution Service in Cases Arising from a Death in Custody,* (2003) http://www.lslo.gov.uk/pdf/deathincustody.pdf http://www.cps.gov.uk/publications/others/agdeathscust.html

Her Majesty's Inspectorate of Constabulary, *Winning the Race: Embracing Diversity,* (Home Office, London, 2001).

Her Majesty's Inspectorate of Constabulary, *Policing London "Winning Consent" A Review of Murder Investigation and Community & Race Relations Issues in the Metropolitan Police Service,* (Home Office, London, 2000).

Holdaway, S, *The Racialisation of British Policing. Black or White?,* Macmillan Press Ltd (Basingstoke, 1996).

Home Office, *A Strategy for Improving Performance in Race and Diversity 2004–2009. The Police Race and Diversity Learning and Development Programme,* (Home Office London 2004).

Home Office, *Stephen Lawrence Inquiry. Home Secretary Action's Plan. Second*

Annual Report on Progress, (Home Office London 2001).

Home Office, *Lawrence Steering Group 5th Annual Report 2003–2004*, (Home Office London 2004).

Home Office, *Lawrence Steering Group 6th Annual Report 2005*, (Home Office London 2005).

Home Office, *Reforming the Coroner and Death Certification System. A Position Paper*, (The Stationery Office, Norwich, 2004) http://www.archive2. official-documents.co.uk/document/cm61/6159/ 6159.pdf

Home Office, *Stephen Lawrence Inquiry: Home Secretary's Action Plan*, (Home Office, London, 1999).

Home Office, *Stephen Lawrence Inquiry: Home Secretary's Action Plan. Second Annual Report on Progress,* (Home Office, London, 2001).

Home Office, *Stephen Lawrence Inquiry: Home Secretary's Action Plan. Third Annual Report on Progress,* (Home Office, London, 2002).

Home Office, *Training in racism and cultural diversity,* Home Office Development and Practice Report (London, undated).

House of Lords & House of Commons, *Joint Committee on Human Rights – Third Report,* Session 2004 – 05 http://www.publications.parliament. uk/pa/jt200405/jtselect/jtrights/15/1502.htm

House of Lords & House of Commons, *Joint Committee on Human Rights Deaths in Custody - Third Report. Volume 1,* Session 2004-05, (The Stationery Office, London 2004) http://www.parliament.the-stationery-office.co.uk/pa/jt200405/jtselect/jtrights/15/15.pdf#search =%22Deaths%20in%20custody%22

Inquest, *Criminal Trial of 10 West Midlands Police Officers,* Press Release 5 May 2006 http://www.inquest.org.uk/

Inquest, *Death in Police Custody. Report on the death of Christopher Alder. Humberside Police 1998,* http://www.inquest.org.uk/

Inquest, *Family devastated after acquittal of police officers in Mikey Powell case,* Press Release 2 August 2006, http://www.inquest.org.uk/

Inquest, *How the Inquest System fails bereaved people. Inquest's Response to the Fundamental Review of Coroner Services,* (Inquest, London, 2002) http://inquest.gn.apc.org/pdf/how_the_inquest_system_fails_bereaved _people.pdf

Inquest, *Kwame Wiredu: Black Death in Stoke Newington: Inquest begins*, Press Release Tuesday 11 October 2005, http://inquest.gn.apc.org/pdf/2005/Kwame_Wiredu_Inquest_begin_PR_111005.pdf#search=%22B lack%20%2B%20Stoke%20Newington%20%2B%20death%22

Inquest, *Paul Coker – Another death in Metropolitan Police Custody*, Press Release 22 August 2005, http://inquest.gn.apc.org/pdf/2005/Paul% 20Coker%20INQUEST%20statement%20August%202005.pdf

Inquest, *Racial discrimination and deaths in custody: report to the United Nations Committee on the Elimination of all Forms of Racial Discrimination (CERD)*, (Inquest, London, 1996).

Inquest, *Deaths of Black, Minority and Ethnic People in Custody. Inquest's Submission to the Stephen Lawrence Inquiry 1998*, (Inquest, London, 1998), http://inquest.gn.apc.org/pdf/Deaths_of_Black_Minority_and_Ethnic _People_in_Custody_1998.pdf

Inquest, *Unlawful killing verdicts and prosecutions*, http://www.inquest.org.uk/

Institute of Race Relations, *Deadly Silence. Black Deaths in Custody*, Institute of Race Relations (London, 1991).

Jones, T, and Newburn T, *Widening Access: Improving Police Relations with Hard to Reach Groups*, Police Research Series Paper 138 (Home Office, London 2001).

Leigh, A, Johnson, G, and Ingram, A, *Deaths in Police Custody: Learning the Lessons*, Police Research Series Paper 26 ed. Laycock, G, Home Office (London, 1998).

Luce, T, *Death Certification and Investigation in England, Wales and Northern Ireland – The Report of a Fundamental Review 2003*, (The Stationery Office, London 2003) http://www.archive2.official-documents.co.uk/document/cm58/5831/5831.htm

Macpherson, W, *The Stephen Lawrence Inquiry*, HMSO (London, 1999).

Marlow, A, and Loveday, B, 'Race, policing and the need for leadership' in, *After Macpherson. Policing after the Stephen Lawrence Inquiry*, Ed Marlow, A & Loveday, B, Russell House Publishing (Lyme Regis 2000) pp. 1–14.

Metropolitan Police Authority, *Stop and Search: A Community Evaluation of Recommendation 61 in the London Borough of Hackney*, (The 1990 Trust 2004)

McLaughlin, J. E, and Murji, K, 'After the Stephen Lawrence Report', *Critical Social Policy*, Vol. 19, No. 3, (1999), pp.371-385.

Neyroud, P, and Beckley, A, *Policing, Ethics and Human Rights* Willan Publishing (Cullompton, 2001).

Police Complaints Authority, *Safer Restraint* (Police Complaints Authority, London, 2002).

Police Leadership and Powers Unit, Home Office, *Deaths in Police Custody. Statistics for England and Wales, April 1999 to March 2000,* (Home Office, London).

Police Leadership and Powers Unit, Home Office, *Deaths in Police Custody. Statistics for England and Wales, April 2000 to March 2001,* (Home Office, London).

Police Leadership and Powers Unit, Home Office, *Deaths in Police Custody. Statistics for England and Wales, April 2001 to March 2002,* (Home Office, London).

Police Leadership and Powers Unit, Home Office, *Deaths during or following Police Contact − Statistics for England and Wales April 2003 − March 2004,* (Home Office, London).

Police Leadership and Powers Unit, Home Office, *Analysis of Ethnic Minority Deaths in Police Custody,* (Home Office Communications Directorate, 2004).

Quinton, P, Bland, N, and Miller, J, *Police Stops, Decision-making and Practice,* Police Research Series Paper 130 (Home Office, London, 2000)

Qureshi, F, and Farrell, G, 'Stop and search in 2004: a survey of police officer views and experiences', *International Journal of Police Science and Management,* http://hdl.handle.net/2134/779.

Reiner, R, *Chief Constables: Bobbies, bosses or bureaucrats?* (Oxford University Press, Oxford, 1992).

Reiner, R, *The Politics of the Police,* Oxford University Press (Oxford 2000).

Rowe, M, *Policing, Race and Racism,* Willan Publishing (Cullompton, 2004).

Scarman, Lord, *The Scarman Report. The Brixton Disorders 10−12 April 1981,* Penguin Books (Harmondsworth, 1981).

Smart, H, *Blackstone's Custody Officer's Manual,* (Oxford University Press, Oxford, 2006)

Starmer, K, Strange, M, and Whitaker, Q, *Criminal Justice, Police Powers and Human Rights,* Oxford University Press (Oxford, 2001).

Stuart, M, and Cragg, R, *Race and Diversity Training,* National Learning Requirement (Home Office, London, 2004).

Taylor, S, 'The Scarman Report and explanations of riots' in, *Scarman and After. Essays reflecting on Lord Scarman's Report, the riots and their aftermath*, ed. Benyon, J, Pergamon Press (Oxford, 1984) pp. 20 -36.

United Kingdom Parliament, *Joint Committee on Human Rights – Third Report*, http://www.publications.parliament.uk/pa/jt200405/jtselect/jtrights/15/1502.htm

Ure, J, 'Police accountability in custody management: creating the climate' in, *Deaths in Custody. International Perspectives*, ed. Liebling, A, and Ward, T, Whiting & Birch Ltd (London, 1994) pp.175 - 195.

Vogt, G. S, and Wadham, J, *Deaths in Custody: Redress and Remedies*, Liberty (2003), http://www.liberty-human-rights.org.uk/resources/articles/pdfs/liberty-inquest-booklet.pdf

Woodcock, J, Maisels, J, Hudspith, D, and Irani,° D, *Deaths during or following Police Contact – Statistics for England and Wales April 2002 – March 2003*, (Home Office, London).

STATUTES

The Coroner's Act 1988

Human Rights Act 1998

Police and Criminal Evidence Act 1984

The Terrorism Act 2000

WEB SITES

http://www.acpo.police.uk/about_pages/free.html

http://www.archive2.official documents.co.uk/document/cm58/5831/5831.htm

http://www.archive2.official-documents.co.uk/document/cm61/6159/6159.pdf

http://www.centrex.police.uk/cps/rde/xchg/SID-3E8082DF B84588E3/centrex/root.xsl/home.html

http://conventions.coe.int/Treaty/en/Treaties/Html/005.htm

http://www.cps.gov.uk/publications/others/agdeathscust.html

http://www.dca.gov.uk/legist/coroners_draft.pdf

http://www.guardian.co.uk/lawrence/Story/0,,941199,00.html#article_continue

http://hdl.handle.net/2134/779

http://www.inquest.org.uk/

http://inquest.gn.apc.org/pdf/how_the_inquest_system_fails_bereaved_people.pdf

http://inquest.gn.apc.org/pdf/inquest_AR2004.pdf

http://inquest.gn.apc.org/stats_police.html

http://inquest.gn.apc.org/data_black_deaths_in_police_custody.htm

http://inquest.gn.apc.org/pdf/Deaths_of_Black_Minority_and_Ethnic_People_in_Custody_1998.pdf

http://inquest.gn.apc.org/pdf/2005/Kwame_Wiredu_Inquest_begin_PR_111005.pdf#search=%22Black%20%2B%20Stoke%20Newington%20%2B%20death%22

http://inquest.gn.apc.org/data_deaths_in_police_custody.html

http://www.met.police.uk/diversity/PDF/Bexley%20Interim%20Report.pdf#search=%22Home%20Office%20Purpose%20of%20Diversity%20Training%22

46

http://www.lslo.gov.uk/pdf/deathincustody.pdf

http://www.opsi.gov.uk/ACTS/acts1998/19980042.htm

http://www.parliament.the-stationery-office.co.uk/pa/jt200405/jtselect
/jtrights/15/15.pdf#search=%22Deaths%20in%20custody%22

http://police.homeoffice.gov.uk/news-and-publications/publication/
operational-policing/deaths1999.pdf?view=Binary

http://police.homeoffice.gov.uk/news-and-publications/publication/
operational-policing/deaths2000.pdf?view=Binary

http://www.publications.parliament.uk/pa/jt200405/jtselect/jtrights
/15/1502.htm

http://www.publications.parliament.uk/pa/cm200506/cmhansrd/cm
060508/text/60508w30.htm#60508w30.html_spnew0

http://www.statistics.gov.uk/cci/nugget.asp?id=273

http://www.sussex.police.uk/about_us/race_equality_scheme/Sussex
PoliceDiversityStrategy.pdf

ANNEXE

Schedule of Questions
Diversity training undertaken since the
Stephen Lawrence Inquiry

Transcription 1 (p.51)
A Female Police Constable in her late twenties.

Transcription 2 (p.54)
A Male South Asian Police Constable in his late thirties.

Transcription 3 (p.57)
A Female Detective Police Constable in her early thirties.

Transcription 4 (p.61)
A Male Police Constable in his late forties
from the Leicestershire Constabulary.

Transcription 5 (p.65)
A Male Police Constable in his mid forties
from the Metropolitan Police.

Transcription 6 (p.69)
A Male Policeman linked to the Black Police Association.

*Interviews were recorded with an Olympus WS-100
Digital Voice Recorder and then transcribed.*

SCHEDULE OF QUESTIONS

1. Can you tell me what you understand by diversity training?

2. Do you know what the diversity training unit is?

3. Have you had any diversity training?

4. What purpose did you think it had?

5. Were the trainers both internal and external?

6. Did the trainers come from a diverse range of religious and ethnic backgrounds?

7. Were the trainers both men and women?

8. What factors do you think are critical for building a racial awareness programme?

9. Did you also receive any human rights training?

10. Was this linked in with the diversity training?

11. Do you believe that the training you received is relevant to you as a police officer?

12. Do you believe the training you received is relevant to the police force as a public body?

13. Can you say if this has helped with custody situations involving minority ethnic groups?

TRANSCRIPTION 1

A female police constable in her late twenties.

Interviewer: Right let's see if this is recording.

Female Police Constable: Bla Bla Bla

Interviewer: I expect you are more used to this than I am. The first question I wanted to ask was Can you tell me what you understand by diversity training?

Female Police Constable: Uh yes it's um being taught about minority groups and the different ways in which they um interact with the rest of the community and how we as police officers are to interact with them and the diversity training that I've had it just tells you about different groups and issues that they have and issues that you may encounter while dealing with them.

Interviewer: Right do you know what the diversity training unit is?

Female Police Constable: Ummmm No probably not.

Interviewer: OK have er you had any diversity training personally?

Female Police Constable: Yeah not at Hendon. I was at Hendon four years ago. Not really since then. I don't think.

Interviewer: Er what purpose do you think the training had?

Female Police Constable: Um. I think it helped me understand a few more issues. Um that the different sets of people that live in London have. Um they said about Muslims they like to bury their dead within um a certain amount of days and if we were dealing with like a murder inquiry we like to keep hold of the body for um longer to deal with um forensics and um autopsy on the body and they'd want the body back before then to bury it and we were taught about dealing with issues like that and try to talk to them and say we'd have to hold on to the body longer and to try and find the people who had killed them and stuff. Um taking off shoes when we entered a house as a mark of respect

Interviewer: Um were the trainers that you had both internal trainers and external people drawn from the communities?

Female Police Constable: Yeah at Hendon we had just had our teachers that taught us and we had people lay visitors come in from different communities. We had a gay guy come in from the LGPT community, a black guy come in and umm and I think yeah we had a

Muslim guy come in as well but I know Hendon's different now. My partner has just finished her training at Hendon and um they've got special trainers there now that are um that go on diversity courses and they are police officers but they are like highly trained and she said that she'd never had anything like it and it was like she's got loads of boys in her class and they were quite big boys and everyone's cried at least once through the week's training that they had. They said it was really moving and I didn't have any of that. So I think the training they've got now is better but mine was OK I guess but was I suppose Hendon's a weird place. It's eighteen weeks of intense training and it's certainly a lot to take in and it was in the first couple of weeks so by the end of it you are worrying about everything else more than what we learnt in the first couple of weeks really.

Interviewer: Were the trainers both men and women?

Female Police Constable: Yes

Interviewer: OK. Have you received further on-going training since then?

Female Police Constable: No

Interviewer: No. Um Do you feel this has any practical approach any practical purpose to your police work on a day to day basis?

Female Police Constable: Um ...Not no Ummm I guess so Yeah

Interviewer: Umm What factors do you think are critical personally to holding a racial awareness programme?

Female Police Constable: Umm Learning to interact better with the communities. Um Sorry can you ask the question again?

Interviewer: Yes, of course. What factors do you think are critical for building a racial awareness programme?

Female Police Constable: Um I'm not sure.

Interviewer: That's fine. Did you get any human rights training?

Female Police Constable: Umm. No not really. We've got a mnemonic that we use called PLAN which is proportionate legal um Oh you're testing me now proportionate legal and I can't remember what the A and the N stands for. That's all to do with um human rights and um oh the N's necessary Oh an I think the A's accounts for. Those are the sorts of things that we are looking for when we arrest someone Is it necessary to arrest that person? Be accountable for those for those things. So that's all on human rights that I know really.

Interviewer: Um was this er training, the human right training, linked to diversity training?

Female Police Constable: Um No I don't think it was.

Interviewer: I apologise for this pause.

Female Police Constable: That's OK

Interviewer: Yeah I want to ask a question again. Do you believe that the training you received was relevant to you as a police officer? It's just part of the ordering of the questions which you are encouraged to do. I just wanted to ask if you had any other thoughts.

Female Police Constable: Yeah I think it is important that we learn about different societies so that when we come across them it is that we are more aware of their needs and issues. I do think that we do need this training. Definitely.

Interviewer: Um Do you believe it has any relevance to the police more widely as a public body as a service that it provides to the community?

Female Police Constable: Yeah definitely. Definitely and especially in London coz it's so diverse here every community that you could imagine here. We've have a lot of tourists as well come here from all different countries. Yeah definitely.

Interviewer: Can you say if this is helpful for instance in custody situations involving a minority or ethnic minority groups?

Female Police Constable: Custody situations. I don't think I've really dealt with anything in custody. Oh yeah I arrested four Asian guys on the Eid Festival. Um was it the Eid Festival? I can't remember now but they were fasting and they had to eat at midnight and so no they weren't very impressed that we had arrested them in the first place but they um. But yeah we had to deal with that situation because they were really hungry by midnight. So we had to feed them That's about all I can think about. We have different meats and meals and stuff. Muslims can't eat and so they have to have halal meat and stuff and so. Yeah that's the only situation I think I have come across.

Interviewer: OK that's very helpful. That's all, thank you very much, that's very helpful

Female Police Constable: Alright

TRANSCRIPTION 2

A male South Asian police constable in his late thirties.

Interviewer: Right ..... do you want to start the interview now then?
Policeman: Yeah yeah
Interviewer: OK can you tell me what you understand by diversity training?
Policeman: Diverse. What. Yeah. It's basically um understanding the multicultural make-up of London really. And understanding other people's race, culture, faith religion.
Interviewer: Um do you know what the diversity training unit is?
Policeman: What within the Met? Um, not too sure. It's either based at the DCC 4 I think they normally deal with the training packs and training programmes.
Interviewer: Have you had any diversity training yourself?
Policeman: I have um although it was. I think the last one I did must have been about three years ago.
Interviewer: Er what purpose do you think this training had?
Policeman: Personally I don't think it had a massive impact on me because I'm born and bred in London and I've grown up with the various cultures anyway. So for me it did not really have a massive impact. Although I was able to give my own input on my faith and culture. So.
Interviewer: Were er were the trainers you had both internal trainers and external trainers.
Policeman: Yeah I think there was one external one I remember there was one internal who was a police sergeant. I think it was.
Interviewer: Did these er Did these trainers come from a range of er religious and ethnic backgrounds?
Policeman: Ummm As far as I remember one was white and the other one was Afro-Caribbean background origin.
Interviewer: Were they both men and women?
Policeman: Yeah
Interviewer: Have you received any further on-going training since the initial programme?
Policeman: No. I have to say that most that my understanding is that most of diversity training takes place on boroughs whereas when you

move into squads and specialist departments to me it seems to stop when you come out of borough policing.

Interviewer: Do you feel this had any practical application, the training?

Policeman: Um from when I last did it or in general?

Interviewer: In general

Policeman: Practical. I'm not sure how to answer that really.Um I think as the years have gone by I think the Met is getting better and better. There's just so much literature information dotted all round police stations and police buildings. You've got your staff associations. . . . . It's everywhere. It is everywhere. So people's understanding is vastly improved.

Interviewer: Um what factors do you think are critical for building a racial awareness programme?

Policeman: Engaging with the community is the only way you are going to do it and getting feedback from the community about what they want.

Interviewer: Did you also receive any human rights training?

Policeman: Sorry

Interviewer: Any human rights. Did you receive any human rights training?

Policeman: Oh yes yes. We um. We did get human rights training. What is officially incorporated into British law by um Mr. Blair. That's Tony Blair. Hm.

Interviewer: Was this linked to the diversity training that you received?

Policeman: No I think it was completely unrelated. Diversity training was on-going.

Interviewer: Do you believe that the training you received was relevant to you as a police officer?

Policeman: What human rights?

Interviewer: No the whole programme of training.

Policeman: Oh yeah. You always need constant ongoing training because you are always change. Situations change.

Interviewer: And you feel that the human rights and diversity training were both useful?

Policeman: Oh yeah yeah definitely.

Interviewer: Do you believe that diversity training has any relevance to the police as a public body as a service to the public?

Policeman: Well yeah because it has a massive impact because it's obviously the people we serve by consent.

Interviewer: OK

Policeman: And as London is such a multicultural. Well it must be the most multicultural city in the world at the moment. So yeah you need that training.

Interviewer: Er Can you say if this has helped the diversity training with custody situations involving minority ethnic groups.

Policeman: Yeah without a doubt. Um because when say someone from an ethnic background or hasn't got a good grasp of English and has just come into the country he goes through the custody suite there's always a big binder of the various different languages that sets out their rights what their entitled to and things like that The interpretation list that's available on um what we call the cab machine um is massive. It's a hell of a lot bigger what it was when I first joined the job. There's always people obviously since the EC countries all the integration and new EC countries or new countries coming into the EC and it's odds on that you are going to get waves of people coming to the country purely for the economic benefit and obviously does represent opportunities for those engaged in criminality and when obviously they're arrested for whatever they do then obviously if they can't speak very good English they are going to need their rights read in their own language or in their own language. And that's all available.

Interviewer: Well that's very helpful then. Thank you very much. We'll that stop now.

TRANSCRIPTION 3

A female detective police constable in her early thirties.

Interviewer: Um right the first question I wanted to ask you er is can you tell me what you understand by um diversity training?

Female Police Constable: Um I understand it be creating awareness um about people's um ethnicities, cultures, backgrounds, sexuality I mean a lot of things to be honest but basically um making people aware um of the needs of other people basically um and about yeah I would have said culture about religion being aware of sensitive aspects of that that you need to be aware of in every day policing.

Interviewer: Do you know what the diversity training unit is?

Female Police Constable: Um No I have heard of it but I don't know what they do or anything like that

Interviewer: OK. Have you had any diversity training personally?

Female Police Constable: Yes

Interviewer: What purpose do you think this training had?

Female Police Constable: Um again it just sort of highlights issue people aware um of the the fact that policing in general today is is you are catering to a very diverse community and that like I said it can go back from and it can educate people on cultural awareness about people's backgrounds, about their religion about the environment people come from um and just you know making you aware so that sexuality race um and being just being aware of the community as diverse and that's as much as I've only had basic training in diversity, but yeah.

Interviewer: OK were the trainers you had both internal trainers and external trainers?

Female Police Constable: I think it was just internal. Yes it's always been internal trainers whenever it's been on diversity.

Interviewer: OK um did the trainers did they come from a range of religious and ethnic backgrounds?

Female Police Constable: No

Interviewer: OK. Were they both men and women?

Female Police Constable: Yes

Interviewer: OK er have you received any further on-going training since the initial programme?

Female Police Constable: When you say initial programme what

Interviewer: The one you alluded to earlier the training that you received initially.

Female Police Constable: Yeah I have.

Interviewer: OK

Female Police Constable: Yep

Interviewer: Do you feel that this training had any practical application?

Female Police Constable: Ummm It's a tricky question. No I don't think it does. I don't think any training um to be honest um can um increase somebody's knowledge about diversity in the community I think it's you know it's very much known that we live in a diverse community. I don't think any training can prepare me for being better equipped to dealing with people that live in a diverse community.

Interviewer: OK that's fine. Um what factors do you think are critical for building a racial awareness programme?

Female Police Constable: Um you say racial awareness programme. What I mean what do you mean by that?

Interviewer: Er basically to be aware of different um ethnic er and racial backgrounds in order for people to appreciate er the differences between different races and er different cultures um.

Female Police Constable: So what's the question again? Would that help create awareness?

Interviewer: No, no. I am asking what factors do you think are critical for building an understanding of racial differences and an understanding of different races and ethnic groups?

Female Police Constable: Factors um? Well working with people, communicating with people, which is what police officers do on a daily basis anyway. Um you know listening to their opinions about you know their problems about their opinions on stuff um yeah

Interviewer: OK that's fine. Um Did you also receive any human rights training?

Female Police Constable: Um we do. Yeah we do receive human rights training and that's in relation to basic human rights custody procedures. Yeah there is a lot of that. You know that's filtered through everything we do pretty much.

Interviewer: OK was this linked into the diversity training?

Female Police Constable: Ummm I can't um I can't remember. It's hard to say. I don't know.

Interviewer: That's fine. Um. Do you believe the training you received is relevant to you personally as a police officer?

Female Police Constable: Um yes some of it is. Um yes some of it is coz you get um you know you get training on people's sexual highlighting sexuality and so that relates to me and also training on women within the workforce and that obviously relates to me so yes.

Interviewer: OK. Um. Do you believe this has any relevance to the police as a public body?

Female Police Constable: What

Interviewer: The training

Female Police Constable: Has relevance to the police?

Interviewer: As a public body as a service it provides to the community.

Female Police Constable: Not sure I understand the question

Interviewer: When I refer to public body um.

Female Police Constable: I know what you mean by a public body. I just ....

Interviewer: Well basically it's just something which interacts with the community er It's not a private organisation but as an organisation which has er its obvious function and outreach is into er the public sector and not into private lives. I was just wondering er do you believe it has any relevance broadly to the police as that sort of organisation which has its main its main interplay is between citizens and the the organisations in the capacity within citizens.

Female Police Constable: Yep

Interviewer: Do you believe that there is that there is er that diversity training and human rights training has any relevance to the police as a public body in the instance that I have just described?

Female Police Constable: Absolutely. Of course. It goes without saying that if we are a public body we are accountable and yes we need to make sure that we have knowledge of all sectors of society in that we are being fair and treat people equally um within a very diverse community. I think we know that. I think and I do think that it's very applicable to the police to have diversity training. It's very important and that's why we have it.

Interviewer: Right. That's fine. Uh. Just one final question. Um can you say if this training, the diversity training has helped with custody situations involving minority ethnic groups?

Female Police Constable: I don't think it does and the reason being is because everybody that comes into custody has the same rights and, you know, people have different problems or concerns when they come into custody and they are dealt with on an individual basis. So whether diversity training does that I don't think so. I think me as a person treating people equally and with respect to their needs and whatever problems I come across with that individual person in custody I deal with it on a one-to-one basis. I don't deal with it on the fact that I'm listening to or remembering my diversity training.

Interviewer: That's very helpful. No we'll just stop it now and replay it to see if we've actually recorded anything.

TRANSCRIPTION 4

A male police constable in his late forties from the Leicestershire Constabulary.

Interviewer: Right can you tell me what you understand by diversity training?

Male Constable: Um. It is basically looking at um different cultures um and something that might be totally non-acceptable to to one culture and its impacts on how it effects another and bearing having having that um keeping that in mind when dealing with people from different uh backgrounds as to what they perceive and how they perceive you and anything that may or may not effect them; to be looking to having a more broader understanding of er differences in cultures so that you can adapt to each of them to do your job.

Interviewer: OK. Do you know what the diversity training unit is?

Male Constable: Not really. I know it exists. But I don't know how much input they have um I understand it's it's it's at multi-level too because they feed into Chief Constables, senior management teams and they also feed into training and new people new officers coming in. So it's like it's filtered in at the top of the system and comes down and filtered in at the bottom to work up. So it's not just aimed at one particular level. Actually what they cover, how they apply it, implement it.

Interviewer: OK. Have you had any diversity training personally?

Male Constable: Ummm Yes. Umm as to it's Once you've um out of probation um there's very little time for training actually going back into a teaching environment. A lot of it will be self-teach, booklets handouts, somebody coming round giving short talk for half an hour, explaining the basics, self teaching packages on computers. So that's as much as it gets to you.

Interviewer: What purpose do you think the diversity training had?

Male Constable: Ummmm. It's to. The purpose is to help us do a better job and to communicate with the mass populace. It can be perceived as criticism in that you are not doing your job right. Um and that was one of the biggest issues when the Stephen Lawrence Inquiry came out and the phrase "Institutionally Racist" came out. So the officers thought they were being criticised as being racists and they would not go out and do the job because they feared they would be if they were working in an Asian community and stopped eight Asians they were going to be accused of because they saw it as every officer in your work should be a mixture, how many arrests you made how many people you report should should form a match of the of the make-up of the population and if you was out of that not in synch with it you was deemed to be um well racist yourself. That was the biggest thing that came out and trying to get that over to some um officers was a bit difficult.

Interviewer: OK. That's fine. Um anything else. Did I interrupt you in full flow then?

Male Constable: No Fine. No.

Interviewer: Um were the trainers you had, were they both internal and external your trainers?

Male Constable: I'm trying to think. We. I remember when it came up. I think we had half a day's input or something on this as in that you had to attend because it was a big issue at the time. Um I think it was all done in-house. Um having said that there has been some recent training within the last um two to three years that an outside agency's been employed Um with professional actors. And they go away and research incidents and then um act them out in front of you playing the part and the roles of. They've been out and interviewed different people from different backgrounds um drug users, alcoholics, different backgrounds, old, young and they would then recreate the situation. It puts over their feeling to us. It was really interesting as to how people and officers responded to that. It's also done at a different level that there was um constables and sergeants at one level and then inspectors and above on another course and the feedback as to how it went back into to senior management.

Interviewer: Right.

Male Constable: And there was the biggest thing that came out of that was um there was a lack of trust between er senior management and the guy that's down the street. And they found that as soon as their friends went up the promotion ladder they seemed to change and their priorities changed um and it was a great mistrust.

Interviewer: Right.

Male Constable: But actually the training that training that training was. No that was I'm not sure that was actually diversity or I can't remember how they titled it. But it did cover a lot of areas and it was um aimed at giving us input from all different um breakdowns of people in society.

Interviewer: Right. Um. Did the trainers, did they come from different religious and ethnic backgrounds?

Male Constable: Yes. Yeah. Not specifically um I think it's just the make-up of the police service at this time. It's to there are officers in it from different backgrounds and groups and few of those people are in training so ....

Interviewer: OK So so

Male Constable: No specialist selection for them to do it as I understand.

Interviewer: Right.

Male Constable: But then there are a few people in training from different backgrounds.

Interviewer: Right. Um Were er they both men and women?

Male Constable: Yes.

Interviewer: OK. Um, have you received any further on-going training since the initial training programme the diversity?

Male Constable: Um As I said not as in x amount of people going to a classroom and being updated on diversity training. There is always. It's it's now more self-teach, if any thinks of interest that people need to do there are learning pages and training pages on our computer system. Some of it is as well you have to um sign at the end or initial or whatever to say you've actually read these documents.

Interviewer: Yeah

Male Constable: Um and that's um throughout the whole area of law. The law's changing almost daily. It progresses at a very frantic pace and interpretations of new laws. So probably slightly more on diversity, sex discrimination than law it tends to stick out. Yeah probably a little bit more on that. The law you are actually dealing with day to day. You're keeping up to date with that. So yeah that's the hardest part.

Interviewer: OK. Umm Do you feel the diversity training has any er practical application?

Male Constable: Yes. It it really if you take it on board um it can help you er in dealing with your with the job you've got to do coz I am dealing with different backgrounds and cultures. Umm if if those people see you have a little bit understanding of their needs they tend to be a little bit more open welcoming, rather than here's somebody who doesn't know anything about us. So yes it does help.

Interviewer: OK. Umm. What factors do you personally think are critical for building a racial awareness programme?

Male Constable: Cor that's … It's If it's. It's got to be relevant. It's got to be workable. Um coz a lot of laws that are passed are not workable. They are political laws to please different um aspects of community and the paymasters are the politicians. Um so they please both sides which pass the law. You can't complain that that law is unworkable so if there's anything there it's got to be practical, workable. It's got to be proportional as well. Um because you can't have um one thing overtaking overtaking that then hinders your actual job.

Interviewer: Right.

Male Constable: So So if there are any factors that not yet. It would have to be reasonable, proportional, workable and um relevant.

Interviewer: Uhuh umum Um Did you also receive any human rights training?

Male Constable: Um Yes. Yes. It's again there's an initial input and the first 14 15 weeks at police college everything's being fired at you. Then you've got two years, two years of settling down, doing modules, they go into each one a little bit more.

Interviewer: OK

Male Constable: Just being aware of it and applying it. Um So yeah human rights do come into it.

Interviewer: Um Was the human rights training linked to the diversity training?

Male Constable: Probably. I honestly can't remember this one.

Interviewer: That's fine. Um do you believe the training you received is relevant to you as a police officer?

Male Constable: Yes.

Interviewer: Do you believe the training or the general programme has relevance to the police as a public body as a service that it provides to the community?

Male Constable: Yes, most certainly coz training the training that you are given and certainly different areas and this is one of them will create more discussion amongst officers both one-to-one when you are out on in a car at night on your own um round the briefing table if somebody's read the package and done it and everything. They understand what you mean and there is good communication within the service and anything doesn't quite meet with people with different interpretations.

Interviewer: Just one final question. Can you say if this training, the diversity and human rights training, has helped with um custody situations involving minority ethnic groups?

Male Constable: Umm. You You'd have to say Yes it has helped but it has helped not in one specific leap and bound. It's just an on-going part of making um you being able to do your job better in relation to the backgrounds of people that you are bringing in. Um and it modifies your systems um makes individual officers aware and makes the police service aware. So yes it it has helped but it's it's it's not helped or been greater than any other area that has the system modernised.

Interviewer: OK. That's very helpful. No. Thank you very much

TRANSCRIPTION 5

A male police constable in his mid forties from the Metropolitan Police.

Interviewer: Right. Um. Can you tell me what you understand personally by diversity training?

Male Constable: Um I suppose it's giving people an awareness of all the different sorts of um issues in relation to diversity and primarily showing respect um and people understanding different people's needs.

Interviewer: Um. OK. Um. Do you know what the diversity training unit is?

Male Constable: Within the police service are you talking about or?

Interviewer: Yes

Male Constable: Um I am aware of that unit and they have come out and done presentations um which has been um throughout the organisation. There's been compulsory training um from I think it was Cultural and Community Relations or CC or something like that. I can't remember what the actual phrase was. It was some sort of race relations training we did and then there was that stint on diversity training. Um so I'm aware of the unit. I'm aware it exists. Um, there's been a lot of changes, I think, in the organisation as to which command it falls under now. Um and ah

Interviewer: OK. Do you want to say any more to that question about the er diversity training unit?

Male Constable: No I am aware the unit exists and I am aware that they have done training throughout the Met.

Interviewer: Er have you had any diversity training personally?

Male Constable: Yes.

Interviewer: OK Er what purpose do you think the training had?

Male Constable: Um I think it was to make us more aware of um different communities and cultures within the cosmopolitan largely cosmopolitan area of London that we work in really. So it's just um giving us an understanding of different needs from those communities.

Interviewer: OK. That's fine. Um Were the trainers you had were they both internal trainers and er external trainers?

Male Constable: Um I can't recall now. Um I know um there's been a mixture. I believe the last course I went to which was predominantly run by the Black Police Association funny for them was external trainers.

Um and internal trainers was were also used as well - so a mixture.

Interviewer: OK. Er Were they both er did they come from a range of religious and ethnic backgrounds?

Male constable: Yes . Um I remember one guy was sort of Scottish Indian background. He had quite a diverse background um living up north somewhere in in England. Um I don't I think the other was a white female trainer. So

Interviewer: Um I suppose the next question is less important then. Were the trainers both men and women?

Male Constable: There you go.

Interviewer: Um. Have you received any further on-going training since the initial programme?

Male Constable: Um, yeah the initial programme um there was a second course that I went on which was a week's course. Um I can't recall what the name was. It was run at Bushey, which was not the best place, which is a sports club at the Met police in Hertfordshire. Um um and that was a week an additional course after the initial training.

Interviewer: Umum Er

Male Constable: Oh That wasn't open to everyone though it was it was looking at um minority staff within the organisation predominantly although that window has now opened slightly um to other groups. So that the gay community and females and stuff like that were targeted.

Interviewer: Right. Um. Do you feel the training had any practical application?

Male Constable: Yes. Um I suppose it widened my scope both of understanding of different communities I suppose sometimes we remain rather insular with that sort of look around and holistically see what other people, other organisations, other needs are. And er. So yes it gave me insight.

Interviewer: OK. Er What factors do you personally think are critical for building er a racial awareness programme?

Male Constable: Um. I think initially the environment needs to be considered. Um I would prefer away from a police environment. I think you'll get better response. Um having a mixture of people. Having reasonably large group. There was another training session that was um being looked at by Centrex. Have you heard of Centrex?

Interviewer: Yes

Male Constable: Um and they were looking at that and they started. I went to another course that was here and they cancelled the course because there was only four or five people so you wouldn't have had a big diversity of different opinions. It would just have been a number of people speaking and if you had stronger personalities in the group um we wouldn't have necessarily have got across. Um so I think the venue's important, having a cross of people, um ideally having a dynamic trainer, someone whose going to be interesting to listen to um because I think people can just think Aw not diversity training again and they just get bored with it. So it needs to be interactive um not just, you know, go away breakdown in small groups and, you know, write with a big thick marker pen on a piece of paper and stick it up with some Blue Tack on a wall. It needs a bit more thought to it. Um um when we did the service change policy um the organisation got on board. I think, something called Ten Thousand Volts. Did you hear about that?

Interviewer: No I haven't

Male Constable: Well we got about a room of say 50 or 60 computers laptops and as a team. There's a table with questions put up on a display and you as a team could allegedly anonymously respond back and answer the question and then you'd get the management actually saying "Well OK we can in answer to this do this and this and this. It was an accumulation of information ideas. Yeah, having a dynamic way of um of presenting it rather than just sitting and being front loaded.

Interviewer: Ok. Did you also receive any human rights training?

Male Constable: Yes.

Interviewer: Er was the human rights training linked to the diversity training?

Male Constable: No, um it was I think um was one of those CBT where you actually go on the computer yourself and you have to go through the legislation, the practical issues as a police officer, and how within the work environment um it's going to effect operationally and working and um I think there was a package on the computer that we all had to do, which I did.

Interviewer: OK. Um. Do you believe um that the training you received, the human rights and diversity training is relevant to your role as a police officer?

Male Constable: Yes it is.

Interviewer: OK. Um do you believe it has any relevance to the police more widely as a public body as a service that er it provides to the er community?

Male Constable: Do I believe that it has a more ere r what?

Interviewer: The relevance to the police as a public body.

Male Constable: Relevance. Oh yeah it's important that any changes in legislation where we are going to be dealing with people on a day-to-day basis we need to be made aware of that. Um I often find that we tend to be looking at it right as it is about to be published. The legislation has just come in and I suppose that's when it's most up-to-date but um sometimes it's even once its in place and then we get the training so it can be right at the beginning of its sort of inauguration. So I suppose the criticism it's a little bit late in coming to us.

Interviewer: OK. Um can you say er if this training in the human rights and diversity training has helped er with custody situations involving minority ethnic groups?

Male Constable: Um I am aware um. I'm not a sergeant so I don't know primarily in relation to the way people are looked but I am aware that different boroughs have made contact um through my unit um where they've asked about dietary requirements, prayer facilities, um for those individuals that have been detained. So we are trying to meet the needs of those people. Um show respect to those communities and show an awareness and an understanding of their needs so there has definitely been a change um even certain rooms being set aside and certain food products being stored and certain prayer utensils, is that the word?

Interviewer: Yeah.

Police Constable: Prayer items, like books and headscarves or whatever it might be. So there has been, I think, a dramatic change in the way we consider people from minority groups and um their needs when they come into custody.

Interviewer: OK. That's very helpful. That's all. So thank you very much.

TRANSCRIPTION 6

A male policeman seconded to the Black Police Association.

Interviewer: Right, um Can you tell me what you er understand by diversity training personally?

Policeman: My understanding basically. I've been a police officer for . . . . . . .and the whole idea of diversity training came out of what was originally called Community and Race Relations Training and that stems as a result of race riots that we had. We had the Notting Hill Riots in the late Seventies then we had the Brixton Riots, the race riots not just in Brixton in London but also in Toxteth in Liverpool, Moss Side in Manchester and so forth and as a result of this one of the recommendations by Lord Scarman back in the eighties was that there should be some form of training for officers to understand the community that they police.

Interviewer: Umum. OK. Um. Do you know what the Diversity Training Unit is?

Policeman: Well my understanding is that there's a separate department that deals with diversity training.

Interviewer: OK

Policeman: Even though I prefer um the term that they had before was Race and Diversity because the whole idea of the diversity seems to dilute the whole thing but my understanding is that the diversity unit is a department like any other department in the police services which specifically deals with certain aspects of training within the job, like riot training, um firearms training and so forth. Then you have the Diversity Unit that deals with the what we call now the Six Strands of Diversity.

Interviewer: OK. Have you had any diversity training personally?

Policeman: Um. Well I haven't been an operational officer for a long while. . . . . Um prior to that I remember all divisions going to the Yard um training but it wasn't anything extensive. It might have been a day or so, but nothing extensive.

Interviewer: OK. What purpose do you think this training had?

Policeman: Well man like I said before the purpose of the training is to enlighten staff as to the differing cultures and the different aspects of diversity if you like. Whether it's to do with women. Whether it's to do with sexual orientation, race, disability and so forth and my understanding it's to give a better understanding to police staff or police officers when they actually go on patrol. What they are going to be dealing with because many times we tend to police everybody the same, which should not be the case we should police people um according to their needs.

Interviewer: OK. Um Right. Were the trainers that er you had were they both er internal and external trainers?

Policeman: My understanding at the time it was mainly internal. I know now that they are trying to extend that to external trainers, but at the time they were just police officers doing training. When on the odd occasion they would bring someone in from the outside, maybe someone who is a Rastafarian, for instance, um at that time when we did our training. As I said way back in the late eighties or early nineties.

Interviewer: OK. Um did the er did the trainers come from er a range of um religious and ethnic backgrounds?

Policeman: At that time it was a more concentrated it was more concentrated on race um rather than any other diversity when I did mine service mainly from various backgrounds. As I said it was mainly to do with people of colour rather than anyone else at the time. I can't remember any women talking about women's issues or disability or sexual orientation. At the time it was mainly on race.

Interviewer: Er. It seems like a fairly obvious question in view of what you said. Have you received any further or did you receive any further on-going training after your initial programme?

Policeman: No, not all because after I left and then got seconded to the National Black Police Association as ....then obviously that took its, you know. I was delivering, if you like, training. Yeah. because I do inputs into places like Centrex. I'm not sure if you've heard of that.

Interviewer: Yes, I have.

Policeman: Places like Centrex and help outside many government bodies as well, like for instance, the Prime Minister's Cabinet Office, um the Home Office itself, the Prison Services, et cetera.

Interviewer: OK, Ummm. Actually did I, I think I may have missed this question out. Er Did I ask you this one? Were the trainers both men and women?

Policeman: Oh you asked me for their backgrounds, but no at the time when I remember. I think it was mixed but it was normally delivered by white trainers, white men and white women.

Interviewer: Um. Did you feel that the training had er any practical application for your role as a police officer then?

Policeman: I think at the time the police service was trying to do its best, but I still think they may have missed the point. Um the time at which I did my training it was about you do not call a black person "a nigger" or call an Asian person "a Paki" which did not help because what you then got people were frightened then to talk to people which seem different from them and that was the issue. Now the training that I do I explain to people why is it people get upset if you call them "a nigger" or you call someone "a Paki" what the term means, where its originated from and so forth which is a better way to get someone to understand what they are dealing with rather than telling them not to use certain terminology.

Interviewer: OK. Um What factors do you think er personally are critical for building er racial awareness programme?

Policeman: Well personally I think um that you cannot get someone who has not had the experience to try and translate that to someone else. In other words at the time when we had race relations training er for me it would have been better to have someone who has experienced racism to deliver that to give a better understanding. It's not like teaching geography or physics or science. This is about the experiences that we have. You're a white man. I'm a black man. I'll never know what it's like to be a white man and you have no idea what it's like to be black er to be black. And similar for people of different orientations or genders. And I think this is something that we need to take into consideration. Secondly this subject matter is not something to be glossed over. The impression that I got people just doing it in order to tick their box or to satisfy the government that they've done it rather than really doing it properly. For instance, if you were doing firearms training it would be very intensive or a driving course you know, you know for instance doing the detective course at that time was something like going away for six weeks. Firearms courses were for weeks, driving courses in two weeks. Yet diversity training was for a day a year. Yet that training was much more important than these matters. So you've guessed it.

Interviewer: OK. Um. Did you also receive any human rights training? I don't know if you want to add anything else there because obviously Human Rights Act 1998?

Policeman: Um, I can't remember receiving anything on the Human Rights Act at all. Again the former training was really basic. Um like they were talking about how people feel if you're policing and that sort of thing, but into the depths of the Human Rights Act er No. That wasn't on the agenda at the time.

Interviewer: Um Anything else to add on from that issue seeing you're not an operational officer at the moment just anything anything anything you want to add.

Policeman: On to that matter? No. I If you ask my view about how things are at the moment and whether things are changed as a result of this training I think very little. Again for the mere fact that it wasn't done properly. Many people have made a lot of money out of this diversity training but have they really delivered. I think not and I think we really have to sit down properly and devise decent programmes in order to deliver race relations training. I think one of the best ones I've seen outside of this country was something delivered by a woman called Jane Elliott to do with the Brown Eyes Blue Eyes Experiment she did in the sixties. Now I've seen her recently delivering as a white female delivering to a mainly white audience and that certainly seems to have made an impact on she was delivering. Now to me something like that - more practical, more direct, more letting you know as it is, that's something helpful. As to deliverance from someone like myself or my colleagues it's not just about sharing experiences, but it's also explaining to people a lot of what they don't know about black people because right now a lot of what people know about people of colour, particularly someone like myself of African descent it's all about slavery and you drew that 400 years of my sort of history. We go way way much further than that. Where we, the Egyptians, you know, educated the Greeks and that's how far I go back. Talk about pre-colonisation of African countries, Asian countries and that's the sort of thing that I think you should be aware of because people then will have a better understanding rather than looking at me as a black man and think well I'm a descendant from Tarzan time or from the jungle. Then you know, I'm someone who's had a history.

Interviewer: Yes. The diversity training you received was it linked into a human rights training?

Policeman: No not that I'm aware of. Again I didn't think they went into that depth. It was mainly superficial. It was mainly digging away at the surface. Um that the concerns that the public had was how the police were treating them, for instance, with racial profiling or Stop and Search. Things like that. A bit like what we're Asian folks are going through at this moment travelling on airports. That was mainly about how do you see people. Why do you stop them and of course the laws change from the SUS laws to the Police and Criminal Evidence Act which means you could not you couldn't just stop someone because of the colour of their skin. You have to have reasonable grounds in order to achieve your aim.

Interviewer: Um. Do you believe the training you received um. I'm sorry this is a little repetitive to a question I asked you earlier. Do you believe this training, er I'm drawing obviously on the human rights element here and also on the diversity training er is relevant er to the role you had as a police officer or to the police more generally?

Policeman: It did make a lot of sense to have something of sorts and um but I think with hindsight a mistake was made that it wasn't done properly. I think there was too much of a knee jerk reaction to rush into putting something down as quickly as possible but I thought it should have been rationalised a lot better maybe delivered by people rather outside the police service with a better understanding of the issues rather than giving a docket to a police officer and saying "This is a manual. Go and train" and that wasn't helpful because what you then get, like I said is this mechanical sort of teaching. Don't do this. Don't do that. And then all it does is just end up scaring people.

Interviewer: Right.. Do you believe this sort of training, the diversity and human rights training, um has relevance to the police as a public body?

Policeman: Most definitely and I think this something particularly when we talk about the human rights um because um I think there are a lot of people only see people who are white as humans and the rest of us are sub-humans and I think that's something that needs to be drilled through because it doesn't matter what colour or what you look like, or sexual orientation or gender, you're a human being and if you're treated as such then people should really know about the Human Rights Act.

Interviewer: OK. Just one final question. I mean drawing from your experience and perhaps more generally, um since the new wave of diversity training has come through can you say if diversity training helps or did help in the past um with custody situations involving er minority ethnic groups?

Policeman: I think there was some changes for instance um in the past where it does not matter whether you like it or not we're gone give you the food that's cooked in the canteen and I think a lot of that has changed now. So if say someone who is of Muslim background came into custody now I wouldn't expect them to be getting pork from the menu or anything like that or non-halal food. I think that if someone Jewish that they would get kosher food. Now things like that have changed which goes a long way because you're recognising somebody's faith and yes I did see evidence of that before I left, but as far as diversity is concerned it's much more than about how you feed someone or what prayer room you provide or prayer mat et cetera. It's again the wholeness of how you treat a human being.

Interviewer: OK, that's very helpful. Thank you very much.

BLACK DEATHS IN POLICE CUSTODY

David Oluwale
17 April 1969
In the proximity of Millgarth Police Station

Aseta Sims
1971

Michael Ferraria
10 December 1978
Stoke Newington Police Station

Singh Grewal
2 August 1979
Southall Police Station

Henry Floyd
23 August 1979
West End Central Police Station

Leroy Gordon
20 August 1980
Pershore Police Station

Winston Rose
13 July 1981
A police van

Shohik Meah
6 November 1981
Thornhill Road Police Station Birmingham

Franklyn Lee
20 September 1982

Simeon Collins
10 December 1982
City Road Police Station

Colin Roach
12 January 1983
Stoke Newington Police Station

James Ruddock
14 February 1983
Kensington Police Station

Nicholas Ofusu
6 May 1983

Matthew Paul
6 May 1983
Leman Police Station

James Hall
30 March 1985

John Mikkelson
15 July 1985

Clinton McCurbin
20 February 1987
Wolverhampton town centre

Nenneh Jalloh
24 April 1987

Mohammed Parkit
1 May 1987

Mark Ventour
24 September 1987

Joseph Palombella
October 1987

Oakley Ramsey
25 June 1988

Derek Buchanan
4 September 1988

David 'Duke' Daley
February 1989

Nicholas Bramble
March 1989

Vincent Graham
July 1989

Edwin Carr
12 July 1989

Vandana Patel
29 April 1991
Stoke Newington Police Station

Leon Patterson
21 November 1992
Denton Police Station

Randhir Showpal
19 December 1992
Norbury Police Station

Joy Gardner
28 July 1993
At her home

Mark Harris
10 July 1994
Bristol police station

Shkander Singh
18 September 1994
Stewart Street Police Station, Glasgow

Oluwashiji Lapite
16 December 1994
Police van in Hackney

Brian Douglas
8 March 1995
Kennington Police Station

Wayne Douglas
5 December 1995
Brixton Police Station

Ibrahima Sey
16 March 1996
Ilford Police Station

Ziya Bitirim
April 1996

Donovan Williams
April 1996
Peckham Police Station

Ahmed El Gammal
13 August 1996
Leyton Police Station

George Bosie Davies
7 October 1996
Marylebone Police Station

Herbert Gabbidon
10 January 1997
In custody of Walsall Police

Marlon Downes
23 March 1997
Harlesden Police Station

Lytton Shatton
1 May 1997
Wolverhampton police custody

Christopher Alder
1 April 1998
Queen's Garden Police Station, Hull

Patrick Louis
2 November 1998
Plumstead police custody

Rodney Sylvester
18 January 1999
Tottenham

Robert Allotey
24 January 1999
Wolverhampton police custody

Sarah Thomas
6 August 1999
Stoke Newington Police Station

Asif Dad
16 January 2000
Chelmsford police Custody

Sultan Khan
30 June 2000
Clarence Park, St Albans

Ricky Bishop
23 November 2001
Brixton Police Station

Lee Duvall
14 August 2002
Ladywell Police Station

Mikey Powell
7 September 2003
Handsworth

Kwame Wiredu
30 August 2002
Stoke Newington Police Station

Paul Yorke
2 November 2003
Heathrow Police Station

Paul Coker
6 August 2005
Plumstead Police Station

Azelle Rodney
30 April 2005
Edgeware

Frank Ogboru
26 September 2006
Woolwich police custody

Nadeem Khan
30 June 2007
Burnley Police Station

THIS LIST IS NOT EXHAUSTIVE

INDEX